AIRPORT

AIRPORT

BEHIND THE SCENES OF COMMERCIAL AVIATION

Michael Sharpe ● Philip Birtles ● Graham Duke

PRC

This edition first published in 2001 by
PRC Publishing Ltd,
8-10 Blenheim Court
Brewery Road
London N7 9NY

© 2001 PRC Publishing Ltd
a subsidiary of Chrysalis Books

ISBN 1 85648 601 X

Printed and bound in China

Cover Acknowledgements
Front cover: © Jacques M Chenet/CORBIS
Back cover (top left): Philip J Birtles (see page 116 bottom)
Back cover (bottom left): Philip J Birtles (see pages 172-173 (main)
Back cover (top right): via Peter R March (see pages 110-111)
Back cover (bottom right): Airsys ATM (see pages 124-125)

Previous Page: *Amsterdam Schipol Airport, KLM's home base
as is evinced by the multitude of blue aircraft in this publicity
photograph for the Dutch national carrier.* via Peter R. March

Right: *Dusk at Schipol does not hinder the loading a KLM Boeing
747-300 Combi.* via Peter R. March

Contents

Introduction

Only sixty years ago, air travel was an occasional novelty for many and a regular event for a few. Every flight was considered an adventure—and perhaps a glamorous one, too. That vision of air travel has all but disappeared, replaced by the modern image of air travel as a routine, safe, and comparatively cheap means of spanning the globe. It is by no means universally accessible, and it remains a fact that the larger percentage of the world's population never takes a flight, but the era of cheap air travel has certainly arrived. One can climb on a plane and within a day be on the other side of the world, a three-month journey by ship only two generations past. This freedom of movement is one of the crowning triumphs of the civil aviation industry.

In marked contrast to the apparent decline in the military aircraft industry—which in recent years has witnessed the fall of a number of big players—civil aviation is booming. As International Air Transport Association Director, General Pierre J. Jeanniot reminded delegates at the 2000 International Air Transport Association Conference, today's multi-million dollar global aviation industry is one of the driving forces of globalization, and has a major impact on the global economy.

Deregulation in the U.S. in the late 1970s allowed the industry to mature, and similar, if limited, moves toward deregulation in Europe and further afield have driven the expansion and created today's ultra-competitive market in which airlines are forced to sink or swim. The greatest beneficiary of liberalization has been the consumer, who has seen prices drop in real terms by seventy percent in the past twenty years.

In the first decade of the new millennium, it is forecasted that the number of annual flights will increase by five percent annually, to nearly 2.3 billion. In 1945 the figure was an estimated 9 million, which by 1999 had grown to 1.5 billion. The air freight industry, which in 1945 transported a few thousand tons by air, has been doubling in size every decade since 1970, and in 1999 carried 25 million tons. This sector will experience the most dramatic increase, and combined with the upsurge

Left: *American Airlines' Boeings at Dallas-Fort Worth, the airline's home base. Founded in the 1930s, American is one of the world's best known and largest airlines with an impressive array of old and new aircraft. Here, a mixture of the old—727s (nearest and two furthest)—and more recent—767s.* Peter R. March

in the passenger sector, this will create a demand for a large number of new aircraft, mostly in the mid-size range. The worldwide commercial aircraft fleet will increase to nearly 32,000 by 2019, double its current size, with annual sales of new aircraft worth $10 billion (totaling $1.5 trillion over the twenty-year period). The same growth is predicted for the support service industry, which will be worth an estimated $2.7 trillion over the next twenty years, which is double the amount for actual aircraft sales.

Globally, the industry employed 28 million people in 1998 and provided about $1.36 billion of its wealth. In ten years time, another three million jobs will have been created. Furthermore, international aviation is the prime supporter of international tourism, which presently contributes more than $3.5 billion to the world economy and employs 192 million people, or eight percent of the global workforce.

In terms of aircraft technology, the next generation of passenger airliners will carry yet more passengers over still greater distances. Although most expect high capacity and long range to be the focal points of development, teams in Europe, the U.S., and Japan are studying the next generation of supersonic passenger aircraft and predict that these will have at least twice the capacity, fifty percent more speed, and double the range of the Concorde, while producing only twenty-five percent of the emissions.

Although the economic prospects look bright, and the potential is clear, the industry faces some very real challenges stemming from rising fuel costs, tougher operating regulations governing noise and emissions, and overcrowded airways. Jeanniot put

Below: *Air travel has become a regular form of transport for the people of the world's richer nations. International travel has come a long way from grass strips and walking out to the aircraft from the terminal. Today, passengers don't have to face the elements when they can use retractable passenger gangways, seen here connected to a Sabena Airbus A330 at Brussels Airport.* Peter R. March

voice to these concerns, saying that "our industry continues to be heavily regulated through the sheer inefficiencies associated with the provision...or rather non-provision...of much of the world's aviation infrastructure...and the archaic approach of some governments...who want to continue to control ATCs and airports."

In order to meet these challenges, greater efficiency is needed from the aircraft and over the network of routes that they fly, if the predicted growth in traffic is to be achieved safely, compliantly, and profitably. The application of new technologies is helping to reduce the impact that aircraft have on the environment by increasing the efficiency of engines and airframes, which will in turn have an important influence on fuel costs and thus profitability. This increase in efficiency needs to be matched by an overhaul of the regulatory procedures and increased investment in traffic management, to ensure a healthy future for the civil aviation industry.

In this book, the authors have tried to present the bigger picture, as it were, of this industry. Most of the current crop of aviation reference material focuses on the aircraft or the airports that are the visible face of the industry, but behind them is a vast network of support personnel: mechanics, cleaners, chefs, firemen, baggage handlers, security staff, and air traffic controllers, to name but a few. In fact, eighty percent of the people employed by the industry work in support occupations, but their work is mostly hidden from the public gaze. So in addition to the information on aircraft types and the flight crew, there are descriptions of the maintenance and air traffic control personnel and procedures, the ground handling staff and more, from Check-in to Arrival.

Below: *Some parts of the world have smaller passenger numbers—a more traditional airport view of an Air New Zealand Link Fairchild SA227 at Christchurch, New Zealand.* Brian A. Strickland

Part 1

The Aircraft

The current generation of passenger airliners is the product of ninety years of evolution within the air transport industry. In terms of performance and usage, air travel and aircraft advanced by a more significant degree than any other form of transportation during the twentieth century. If we look at one of the most common airliners of the 1930s, the Douglas DC-2, and its modern equivalent, the Boeing 737, capacity has increased by more than four times, average speed by the same amount, and range by a factor of nearly six. Other relative factors such as efficiency and safety have also improved. Perhaps most significant is the cost to the passenger, which has been reduced to a level at which air travel is affordable to a far greater percentage of the world's population than during the era of the DC-2.

Part 1 provides a broad-brush survey of the main aircraft manufacturers and the main aircraft types that fly passengers from the airports of the world. It then goes on to look at the external and internal workings of modern aircraft before dealing with emergencies, followed by the all-important subject of aero engines and finally, looks at the way modern airliners are constructed.

Left: *Airliner development is at the forefront of industrial design and expertise. Higher, faster, stronger—the motto of the Olympics—relates well to aircraft manufacturers. This is the Airbus A3XX, now the A388. Peter R. March*

THE MANUFACTURERS

Chances are, should you make an intercontinental voyage by air, a shorter trip between Northern Europe and the popular Mediterranean resorts, or else regularly commute on the dense U.S. internal network, you will travel on an aircraft built by one of the two industry giants, Boeing and Airbus. It was not always so clear-cut. In the 1960s there was a plethora of manufacturers engaged in the design and production of commercial jetliners. The number has dwindled significantly, and currently the production of medium to large capacity airliners, which are financially the most important sectors of the global commercial aircraft market, are dominated by the commercial aircraft division of Seattle-based Boeing and the European Airbus Industrie consortium.

Boeing rose to prominence in the commercial jetliner industry with the introduction of the groundbreaking Model 707 in the late 1950s, itself an offshoot of the program to build air-refueling tanker aircraft for the U.S. Air Force. The success of the Model 707 and of the subsequent 727 and 737 cemented the company's reputation. It gambled heavily on the 747 program in the late 1960s, risking much to build the revolutionary wide-body jet, but its gamble ultimately paid off.

During the late 1970s and throughout the 1980s, Boeing dominated the world market, and plentiful orders for its 717, 737, 747-400, 757, 767, and 777 types ensure that the U.S. giant, which swallowed up McDonnell Douglas in 1997 to become the largest aircraft manufacturer in the world, will maintain a leading position for years to come.

Of the other U.S. manufacturers with traditions of commercial aircraft production, McDonnell Douglas, whose name was once as familiar to air travelers as Boeing is today, has been absorbed into its great rival, and Lockheed, which produced one of the best loved of all airliners in the Constellation, ceased production of commercial aircraft after the

Inset: *One of the first generation of commercial jets, the Boeing 707, first flew in 1957. Over forty years later, many are still in service, such as this 707-379C cargo aircraft of the Ugandan carrier Dairo Air Services.* Peter R. March

Left: *Virgin Atlantic Boeing 747-4Q8 G-VFAB, named Lady Penelope, landing at Los Angeles. Virgin has always had an eye for registrations—others in the fleet include -VBIG and -VAST.* Peter R. March

The Aircraft

L-1011 Tristar. Lockheed has since merged with Northrop Grumman.

In the expanding business jet and commuter market, which Boeing has been eyeing, pioneer Learjet (now a subsidiary of Bombardier), Raytheon, Beechcraft, Cessna, Fairchild (now Fairchild Aerospace following the takeover of Dornier), Grumman, Piper, Rockwell, and Swearingen are all active. In the 1ate 1980s and early 1990s, Bombardier Aerospace expanded significantly, acquiring fellow Canadian manufacturers Canadair

(1986) and de Havilland (1992), as well as Shorts of Belfast (1989) and Learjet (1990). Production of its own and Canadair's bizjets, and de Havilland's regional and commuter aircraft continues. The U.S. remains the most important aircraft manufacturing center, the biggest employer of aviation industry personnel, and also one of the most important markets.

Outside of the U.S., Britain took an early post-war lead in the manufacture of commercial airliners with the jet-powered de Havilland Comet, and with the pioneering turboprop Vickers Viscount, but neither aircraft realized its potential. Nor did the Vickers VC-10, the de Havilland Trident, or the elegant Anglo-French Concorde, all products of the 1960s. There have been some limited successes in more recent years, namely the BAC One-Eleven and the BAe146/Avro RJ, the Hawker Siddeley HS125 and HS748, the Britten Norman Islander/Trislander family, and the Shorts aircraft, but large-scale airliner production in Britain has all but ceased.

Left: Brazilian carrier Varig is a significant force in South America and has been a Douglas DC-10-30 user since 1974. Daniel J. March

Below Left: The Douglas DC-3—perhaps better known as the military C-47 Skytrain or Dakota—is the quintessential prop-liner, and the only replacement for a DC-3 is another DC-3. This one is VH-MIN in Australian Dakota National Air colors. Peter R. March

Below: All Nippon Airways Lockheed L-1011 Tristar at Hong Kong's Kai Tak airport. Peter R. March

Above: *European Air Charter BAC One-Eleven 510ED at Lulsgate. The One-Eleven flew first in 1963; the 500 series was built both in the U.K. and by Romaero SA in Romania.* Peter R. March

Right: *British Airways Concorde G-BOAF taking off. The only commercial SST, the future of the Anglo-French joint venture looked uncertain after its July 2000 crash after takeoff from Paris Orly.* Peter R. March

Far Right: *BAe146-200—this one named Pride of Guernsey— of Jersey European, a carrier based at Exeter aiport.* Peter R. March

BRITISH AIRWAYS

Pride of
Guernsey

JERSEY EUROPEAN

The Aircraft

Until the Anglo-French Concorde project, the nationalized French aircraft industry had only produced one commercial jetliner of note—the Sud Aviation Caravelle. Launched in the early 1950s, the Caravelle is now best remembered for the enormous noise generated by its rear-mounted engines! After the Caravelle production line closed, independent French commercial transport aircraft production went into a slump until the 1980s when military aircraft manufacturer Dassault entered the corporate transport market with its Falcon series.

Left: The Sud Aviation Caravelle SE 210 is another of the first-generation jets. This one is in the colors of Air Charter, a subsidiary of Air France. Peter R. March

Below Left: Airbus A330 demonstrator; this long-range airliner first flew in 1987. Airbus had orders for over 250 at the turn of the century. Daniel J. March

Below: Airbus A300B4 of Costa Rican carrier ACS Cargo. This was the fourth freighter conversion by BAe Aviation Services at Filton. Peter R. March

In neighboring Holland, Fokker—which once had a sure footing in the regional airliner market with its turboprop and jet aircraft—has fallen victim to a dwindling order book and ended its ninety-year history of aircraft manufacture. Dornier of Germany continues production of regional jet and turboprop aircraft in partnership with Fairchild, and in Spain, CASA has produced a couple of small regional airliners. The sole Swiss aircraft manufacturer, Pilatus, produces a popular single-turboprop corporate transport and a STOL utility aircraft. Italian manufacturer Piaggio has targeted the same markets.

In contrast to the limited successes enjoyed by European manufacturers acting in isolation to challenge the dominance of U.S. manufacturers, collaboration between France, Germany, Belgium, Italy, Spain, and the United Kingdom in the form of consortium Airbus Industrie has been a singular triumph. Airbus is currently battling Boeing for market supremacy, and in terms of new orders, if not aircraft in current service, it appears to be

taking something of a lead. Airbus was established in the early 1970s, partly at the behest of the respective governments of the consortium member states. France and Germany are the leading partners with responsibility for the manufacture of most of the aircraft structure; Belgium, Italy, Spain, and the U.K. are the junior partners. The Airbus fleet has expanded steadily in the past twenty years and now includes the A300, A310, A319, A320, A321, A330, and A340. The A380, targeted at a predicted market for an aircraft with 800-seat capacity, will become available in five or six years.

Another successful collaboration is Avion de Transport Régional (ATR), owned by a consortium of French, German, and Italian aerospace companies and which produces aircraft for the regional airliner market.

Perhaps less familiar to travelers in North America and Europe are the stable of Ilyushin jetliners, and those of the Tupolev and Yakovlev concerns, which were initiated in the Soviet Union of the 1950s and have achieved notable sales successes in the former Soviet satellite states and in parts of Asia and the developing world. Western observers have often commented on the similarity between certain Western designs and subsequent Russian offerings, but while there may be some suggestion of plagiarism, a history of innovation is also plainly evident. In the post-Soviet era, the Russian aircraft industry, or at least the commercial sector, has struggled to remain buoyant as its traditional markets have been opened up to competition from Airbus and Boeing, and investment has fallen dramatically.

One of only a handful of South American aircraft manufacturers, and currently riding high, is Brazilian Embraer, whose popular business and commuter jets have firmly established the South American company in the commercial aircraft industry.

A new entrant to the bizjet sector is Galaxy, a subsidiary of Israeli Aircraft Industries.

Inset: *Tupolev Tu-204 of Rossiya State Transport seen at Moscow airport. The Tu-204 boasted an EFIS cockpit, winglets and fly-by-wire control system.* Peter R. March

Left: *The Ilyushin Il-18—NATO reporting-name "Coot"—is another 1950s aircraft that is in demand as a freighter.* Peter R. March

The Aircraft

THE AIRCRAFT

Described in brief detail here are some fifty of the important commercial airliners in current service. Although this list is by no means exhaustive, the examples given are fairly representative of the different categories. Many of them have long since ceased production; indeed, a quick review of the current international fleet lists reveals a remarkable preponderance of older Boeing and McDonnell Douglas airfracft, with a sprinkling of evocative names such as BAC and Vickers!

The aircraft are grouped according to range and capacity, and there is a separate section on business jets (some of which have extremely long ranges). One problem with this approach is that aircraft evolution very often results in increased range, as is the case with the 767. Hence, in categorizing the aircraft below, the basic launch model has been taken as the starting point. More space has also been given to describing the more modern types. Engine details may be found in a following section.

The first group covers the ultra long-range, high capacity types. Boeing and Douglas dominated the long-range market in the 1960s with their 707 and DC-8 four-engine jetliners, the aircraft that pioneered long-haul jet travel. Large numbers of 707s are still in operation, the last of them leaving the production line in 1991, some thirty-four years after production began. The 707 was one of the first aircraft to be fitted with turbofan engines and the ultimate production version was the 707-400. Another of the family, the 707-320B, has a range of some 7,630 miles. The four-engine DC-8 was originally produced in five versions, the medium-range Series 10 to 50 and the ultimate production series, the long-range Super 50 and 60. Some examples soldier on as air freighters, a role to which older aircraft are frequently adapted.

At the end of the 1960s, airlines were demanding more capacity and range. None of the current aircraft could meet their needs, as both the Boeing 707 and Douglas DC-8 had reached the limitations of their design evolution, and could not accommodate further stretching or fuel. Boeing recognized a market opportunity and initiated development of the four-engine Model 747, the first of the wide-body twin-aisle jets. This aircraft had a revolutionary effect on intercontinental air travel and across the whole industry. Building it required the construction of the vast Everett plant in Seattle. The 747-100 entered service nearly thirty years ago, and as the 747-400 (first introduced in 1988), the family is still in production. In between there have been -200, -300, and a small number of short SP aircraft, as well as special freighters. Range has been progressively increased from 5,000 miles to 8,000 miles, and maximum capacity to 568 (in the Japanese high-density version of the 747-400), currently the largest number able to be carried by a passenger aircraft. Some early 747s have clocked up enormous mileages: a -200F currently in service

Left: *DHL has a fleet of freighters based at its Cincinati, Ohio home. Here, one of its Douglas DC-8s is seen at Brussels Zaventem.* Peter R. March

Above Left: *Boeing 707, seen in National Air Charters livery as 9J-ADY, flew first in 1965. Its career of 25 years included time spent with its initial customer, Flying Tiger Line, as well as Aer Lingus, Zambia Airways, and Trans Arabian Air Transport, in whose hands it was written off in 1990 following collapse of its undercarriage at Khartoum.* Daniel J. March

Above: *Singapore Airlines Boeing 747-412 9V-SMA coming in to land at Hong Kong. Since May 1990 the -400 has been the only 747 model available to customers.* Peter R. March

Right: *Virgin Atlantic Boeing 747-200 Morning Glory landing in the wet at London Heathrow.* Peter R. March

Far Right: *Cathay Pacific Boeing 747-300 taking off from Hong Kong's Kai Tak airport.* Peter R. March

The Aircraft

with Korean Airlines has a staggering 100,000 hours of air time. Construction at the giant Everett facility near Seattle will continue well into the 21st century with the 747X series, the largest of which will carry 504 passengers in a three-class layout for over 10,000 miles.

The Airbus consortium began to eye the long-haul market in the 1970s, and drew up plans to build a four-engined twin-aisle aircraft to challenge the 747 on sectors that did not require the use of a full 747. These plans were put on ice in the late 1970s, but were brought to the fore again after Boeing announced plans to build the -300 and -400 versions of the 747. In January 1986 the

aircraft received formal designation—A340—and first flew on October 25, 1991. It shares a common basic fuselage with the twin-engine A330, which considerably eases construction; the wing is manufactured by British Aerospace, then flown to Daimler-Benz Aerospace at Bremen and on to the Toulouse assembly plant. Other components come from Aerospatiale, Belairbus, CASA, and CFM. The smallest of the family, the A340-200, typically seats 261 passengers; the largest, the A340-600, seats a maximum of 485. Range is 8,500 miles (A340-500). Orders have been strong, although so far no North American manufacturer has come on board. The next Airbus entry to this market will be the giant twin-deck A380, a four-engine aircraft that will be able to carry between 555 and 880 passengers and which should begin services in 2006.

Slightly lower down the range scale, in the 5,000 to 6,500 miles bracket, the first McDonnell Douglas DC-10 wide-body trijet flew in 1970, and entered service in 1971. Production of the DC-10 ended in 1990, replaced by the MD-11. The DC-10 Series 10 was developed for service on domestic routes of 300 to 3,500 miles, and the later Series 40 and 50 models for intercontinental operations of up to 6,000

Left: *Cathay Pacific Airbus A340 in the skies above Melbourne. The 340 is a very modern aircraft and will be developed and stretched over the next decade into the -500, with a projected range of 8,500 miles, and the -600 intended to carry nearly 400 passengers 7,500 miles.* Peter R. March

Below Left: *JAT McDonnell Douglas DC-10 at London Heathrow.* Peter R. March

Below: *American Airlines McDonnell Douglas MD-11. When Boeing took over McDonnell Douglas, it announced closure of the MD-11 line in 2000.* Daniel J. March

The Aircraft

miles. Maximum capacity is 380. A stretched version of the DC-10 Series 60, designated the MD-11, was developed in the late 1980s to compete with the 747, but it never achieved the same sales success and there is now something of a glut of MD-11s on the secondhand market. Produced in -11, -11ER, -11F, and -11CF (Combi Freighter) versions, the -11ER passenger version has seating for 410 and a range of 7,600 miles. Utilizing a similar tail and fin-mounted powerplant configuration as its rival, the DC-10, the tri-engine wide-body L-1011 Tristar was Lockheed's stab at the U.S. coast-to-coast market, and was first flown in November 1970. Produced in relatively small numbers (250), the first

Left: *Delta Lockheed L1011 TriStar at Atlanta.* Peter R. March

Below Left:*United Airlines Boeing 767-322ER N659UA was delivered in 1993, one of around eight hundred 767s sold.* Peter R. March

Below: *Egypt Air Boeing 777 at London Heathrow. Boeing's first fully fly-by-wire airliner, the impressive 777 will be visible around the world for many years to come.* Daniel J. March

-100 variant was hampered by a limited range of 3,200 miles. The -200 and -500 went some way to rectifying this, having a range of 4,100 miles and 5,900 miles, respectively. Seating capacity is between 360 and 400, depending on the cabin layout.

For the medium to long-range market, Boeing offers versions of its ultra-modern twin-engine 777 and 767. The twin-engine 777 wide-body jet was built to fill the gap between the medium-range 767-300 and ultra long-range high-capacity 747—a market at which Airbus had targeted its A340, and in which the Lockheed Tristar and McDonnell Douglas DC-10 were already entrenched. Boeing spent a great deal of time in garnering customer opinions, and accommodated a large number of them into the final design. The 777 is one of the most advanced aircraft flying today; Boeing boasts that the wing is the most aerodynamically efficient ever developed for subsonic commercial aviation, and its two-man cockpit is packed with advanced avionics equipment. The first aircraft was delivered

Above: *The Ilyushin Il-96T is an all-freight version of the Il-96 passenger airliner developed from the Il-86. Aeroflot's RA-96101 is seen here leaving Moscow.*
Peter R. March

Right: *Lufthansa Airbus A310-203 Recklinghansen at London Heathrow.* Peter R. March

to launch customer United Airlines in May 1995, and the family now includes the 777-200ER, -200LR, 777-300, and 777-300ER, accommodating from 301 to 365 passengers, although a maximum of 550 is possible. Maximum range of the 777-300ER is 6,568 miles. The Seattle company also has two extended-range versions of its Model 767, an aircraft described in detail below. The 767-300ER and 767-400ER, both with ranges in the region of 6,500 miles, will likely be joined by versions of both aircraft with ranges over 7,000 miles.

Airbus competes in this market with the A330, a family of twin-engine wide-body jets that was developed in the early 1990s alongside the A340 for high capacity regional and extended range operations and with which it has much in common. The family includes the -200 and -300 models. A -200 model with three-class seating will typically carry 253 passengers over 6,300 nautical miles.

Illuyshin's Il-96 family, introduced in 1988 and which includes -300, -96M, and -96T versions, is predominantly used by CSR-based operators on long-range routes. The -300M has a 375-plus capacity and range of 6,500 miles.

Of the millions of revenue-earning flights every year, most are over medium-range sectors of between 3,500 and 5,000 miles. It is one of the most demanding areas of the market, one in which operators contest fiercely.

The Airbus A300/310 family of mid-size mid-range airliners was the foundation upon which the company's current success was built, and are the most popular aircraft in this class. Launched in the late 1970s and aimed at regional operators, the twin-engine A300 pioneered the twin-aisle/twin-engine airliner configuration, combining the low cost per seat of the twin-aisle with the low costs of a twin-jet. The family also pioneered digital electrical signaling (fly-by-wire) and fuel-reducing winglets. From the original A300B2/B4 was developed the stretched A310 and A300-600. The A300 has a maximum range of 4,150 nautical miles and maximum capacity of 266 (two-class), while the A310 can carry a maximum of 360. As with other Airbus products, there is also a good deal of commonality between the aircraft structure and systems.

Main competitors to the A300/A310 are Boeing's 767 and 757 twin-engine jets. Boeing announced its intention to develop the two aircraft in 1978, basing the design of the 757 fuselage on the 727. The 767, which had an all-new fuselage, was built first and entered service in September of 1982. The aircraft has been progressively developed since then, resulting in the -200ER, the stretched (21 feet) -300, -300ER, and -300F. This last aircraft has a range of over 6,000 miles and will typically seat 269 passengers. An even longer-range version designated -400ER, with a further fuselage stretch, entered service is August 2000, and the new 7,000-miles-range -400ERX will begin deliveries in 2004.

Its smaller relative, the 757, began revenue services with Eastern Airlines in January 1983. Versions include the -200PF (Package Freighter), -200M Combi, and -300, which has a fuselage stretch of over 23 feet. In a typical three-class cabin layout the 757-300 will seat 240 and maximum range is 3,728 miles.

Although less commonly encountered, Ilyushin's Il-62 is still in widespread service outside Europe.

The Aircraft

Range of the four-engine jet (with the powerplant mounted in tandem pairs on the rear fuselage) is around 4,700 miles, although capacity is rather limited at 200.

The short to medium-range sectors are still the haunt of 1960s veterans such as the Boeing 727, Douglas DC-9, and de Havilland Trident, but the twin-engine Boeing 737 has long ruled the roost. Over a thousand examples of the tri-engine 727 are still in service (Federal Express has over 150 alone), and like the Boeing 717, the DC-9 is still in pro-duction. The less prolific Trident, once the work-horse of European airlines and the queen of the tar-mac at London's Heathrow, is less commonly seen.

Boeing's 737—the world's most popular airliner—began production in the late 1960s and has evolved through -100, -200, -200C, Advanced 200, -300, -400, -500, -600, -700, -800, -900, and most recently 737NG variants, with range from 2,100 miles (-200) to 3,383 miles (-700) and maximum capacity of 103 (-100) to 189 (-900). Orders for the aircraft have surpassed the 5,000 mark, and with development continuing, the air-craft is likely to dominate the sector for years to come. Airbus made a brave foray into the arena with its single-aisle twin-engine A320 family, which includes the A318, A319, A320, and A321. In terms of orders, this family now outsells the 737. Airbus launched the A320 in the early 1980s, and its marketing strategists are quick to point out that, compared to its older competitor, it is a relatively modern design. The smallest member of the family, the A318, is aimed at the 100-seat regional market

Left: *British Airways Boeing 757-236 Killyeagh Castle above Los Angeles. BA is a major supporter of Boeing aircraft with a significant number of 737, 747, 757, 767, and 777 types.* Daniel J. March

Below Left: *Aral Air Ilyushin Il-62M at Moscow with an Il-76 in the background.* Peter R. March

Below: *Until the phenomenal success of the 737, the 727 had sold more than any other airliner, with some 1,800 having been produced from the early 1960s until 1984 when production stopped. This is one in United Airlines' colors.* Peter R. March

The Aircraft

Far Left: *Latest version of the 737 is the -500 delivered first to Southwest in 1990. This is Aer Lingus's EI-CDB St. Albert on approach to Heathrow.* Daniel J. March

Left: *America West Boeing 737-200 at Los Angeles.* Peter R. March

Below: *Braathens Boeing B737-400 coming in to Alicante. Over two thousand 737s have been produced and it is undoubtedly the most popular short to medium-range airliner ever produced.* Peter R. March

The Aircraft

to 220-seat (A321) market, and maximum range is 3,000 nautical miles (A320).

The McDonnell Douglas MD-80/87/90 family, which has now evolved into the Boeing 717 detailed below, was itself a natural outgrowth of the Douglas DC-9 project and is still in widespread use. During the 1960s and 1970s, the twin-jet DC-9 aircraft was the main competitor to the 727, and was produced in -10, -20, -30, -40, and -50 versions with seat capacity between 90 and 140. In the late

1970s, McDonnell Douglas began developing another stretched version of the design, which flew as the DC-9 Super 80 in 1979 and became the MD-80 after a change in the company's designation system in 1983. The MD-80 was destined to become the most successful Douglas commercial aircraft since the DC-3, and was followed into service by the MD-87, and by the advanced MD-90 in 1995, which features a "glass" cockpit, much-reduced fuel consumption, and lower noise emissions. Production of the MD-90 continues at Long Beach, as previously stated, as the Boeing 717.

Ilyushin four-engine Il-76, Il-86, and four-engine Il-18 turboprop fall into the short-range class, as does Tupolev's trijet Tu-154, -204 (-100 series), -214, -224, and -234.

Regional sectors, typically involving fast turnaround, multiple daily flights, and short distances, are best suited to aircraft with a capacity between 30 and 100 and a range of below 2,000 miles, and are thus well suited to smaller twin-jet and turboprop aircraft. Boeing is now competing at the higher end

of the bracket with the 717-200, an aircraft derived from the MD-87-105 (and thus the 1960s vintage DC-9). The twin-jet is the newest addition to the Boeing family has an all-new glass cockpit and revised passenger cabin. Range is 2,209 miles and maximum capacity is 117. A decision on a shortened 86-seat version of the aircraft (717-100X) was still pending in early 2001.

Elsewhere in North America, Bombardier Canadair has its CRJ Series 100, 200, and 70-seat 700 in production, and sister company Bombardier de Havilland continues to build the Dash 8 twin-turboprop in the Q200, Q300, and Q400 variants. Before the merger, de Havilland Canada also built the Dash 7.

Left: *The massive Ilyushin Il-76—NATO reporting name "Candid"—has a max payload of 88,185 lbs.—making it a very useful freighter. This Aeroflot Il-76 is seen landing for an IAT air show.* Peter R. March

Below Left: *AJT Ilyushin Il-86 at Moscow. The Il-86 proved to be short of range and only 104 had been produced when production was halted in the mid-1990s in favor of the Il-96.* Peter R. March

Below: *Trans European Tupolev Tu-204 at Moscow.* Peter R. March

Fairchild Aerospace undertook licensed production of the Fokker F-27 described below in the early 1970s, and has since merged with Dornier of Germany to become the Fairchild Dornier Corporation. Fairchild Dornier has a fairly extensive range of small-capacity regional jet and turbofan aircraft on the market. The Dornier Do228 and Do328 are twin-turboprop aircraft of 19 and 32-seat capacity, and the 728JET family is targeted at the 55-105 market. The family currently includes only the twin-turbofan 728JET, with 70-80 seat capacity, but the 528JET (55-70 seat) and 928JET (100-110 seat) derivatives are due for service entry in 2004 and 2005, respectively.

A relative newcomer is the Brazilian Embraer company, whose 37 and 50-seat ERJ-135 and -145 have captured an important share of the small-capacity regional aircraft market. The modern ERJ is a twin-turbofan aircraft with range of 1,600 miles, which will be complemented by the larger 70-seat ERJ-170 and 98/108-seat ERJ-190 in 2002 and 2004. The company also has the EMB-110 Bandeirante, EMB-120 Brasilia, and

Above: *The Canadair RJ can carry up to fifty passengers around 1,000 miles, making it a handy regional airliner. This one belongs to US Airways Express and is seen at Charleston, SC.*
Peter R. March

Above Right: *Another turboprop-driven STOL airliner, this is an Adria DHC-7.* Peter R. March

Right: *Bombardier bought de Havilland Canada in 1992 and the DHC-8 turboprop became the Dash 8. The Series 400 can carry up to 78 passengers around 1,000 miles.* Peter R. March

The Aircraft

EMB-121 Xingu twin turboprop aircraft in production.

Dutch manufacturer Fokker has now ceased its activities, but was once an established competitor in the market. Beginning with the 1960s vintage F-27 (also built under license by Fairchild) and F-28 twin-turboprop aircraft, through the more modern twin-turboprop 58-seat F-50 of 1985, which was produced in -100 and -300 versions, the company began production of its first jet aircraft, the twin-engine Fokker F-70 and F-100 (1,750 miles/109-plus passengers) in 1986.

With an illustrious background in military aircraft design and production, Saab of Sweden ventured into the regional airliner market with the Saab 340 and 2000, both twin-turboprop aircraft.

Shorts Brothers of Belfast, which also has a famous heritage of military aircraft, built three types of small capacity high-wing twin-turboprop aircraft, the 330, 360, and Skyliner.

Another famous name, Avro, has been resurrected for three small-capacity jet airliners produced by British Aerospace. The RJ70, RJ85, and RJ100 are actually derivatives of the earlier BAe146-100, -200 and -300. British Aerospace unveiled the four-engine high-wing BAe146 aircraft in 1983, and it was replaced by the RJ family in 1993. Capacity of the RJ70/85/100 is 70, 85, and 100-112 and range 1,600, 1,500, and 1,400 miles, respectively. The next version will be the RJX. The previous generation of BAe turboprop aircraft includes the small-capacity (18-seat) Jetstream 31/32, 29-seat

Left: Embraer of Brazil is a leading manufacturer of light airliners and regional jets. This an ERJ-145 of Continental Express, a major Embraer customer, at Houston. Peter R. March

Below Left: The Embraer EMB-110 Bandeirante turboprop carries around twenty passengers and its success—nearly 500 aircraft built between the early 1970s and 1991—helped found the fledgling company. This Bandeirante belongs to the Australian Sunshine Express company. Peter R. March

Below: Known as an aircraft manufacturer from the early years of flying, postwar Fokker has made a name for its regional airliners. This is an F50 of Air Nostrum at Alicante. Peter R. March

The Aircraft

Jetstream 41, and the ATP. Although now defunct, former U.K.-based Britten Norman's Islander and Trislander high-wing twin-turboprops are still faithfully serving on many routes.

The major European regional aircraft manufacturer is ATR, in which Aerospatiale Matra (France), CASA (Spain), and Daimler Chrysler Aerospace (Germany/U.S.)—collectively known as the EADS group—and the Italian Alenia concern have shares. Produced at Naples and Toulouse are the ATR 42 and ATR 72. The twin-turboprop high wing 42 was first flown in 1984 and is available in -300, -320, and -500 versions, all with 46-seat capacity. A lengthened version, designated the -72, with accommodation for another twenty passengers, is

Left: Another successful regional airline manufacturer, Saab followed its 340 with the 2000, a high-speed turboprop with a capacity of over fifty passengers. Peter R. March

Below Left: Air Malta AVRO RJ70. The RJ70 is the BAe-100 relaunched. It can carry up to ninety-four passengers. Peter R. March

Below: The Jetstream 61 is a development of BAe's ATP (advanced turboprop) regional airliner. This Manx aircraft seen at Heathrow is one of a disappointing total of sixty-five built. Daniel J. March

Overleaf: Fairchild Do328-110 of US Air Express, regional partner of US Air. Fairchild took an eighty percent interest in Dornier in 1996, and since then has produced turbofan versions of the Do328. Peter R. March

The Aircraft

available in -200, -210, and -500 versions. Independently, CASA produces the C212 Avíocar and CASA/IPTN CN235.

In the now-independent republics of the former Soviet Union, the 32-seat trijet Yakovlev Yak-40 and its larger stablemate, the Yak-42, are much in evidence, but likely to be replaced by more modern types as and when funds permit. The smaller Yak-40 first flew in 1966 and has a range of 1,250 miles, while the -42 has capacity for 100-120 and a range of 960 miles. One of the newest additions to the Tupolev fleet and planned as a medium-capacity (100-seat) regional aircraft to replace the aging Tu-134 is the twin-jet Tu-334, which began flight testing in 1998.

Once the preserve of an exclusive club, charter services and fractional ownership schemes have helped to bring the convenience and prestige of aircraft ownership to a wider section of the global business community. The market is booming and currently sustains aircraft of broadly differing capabilities: short and long-range, small to medium-capacity, turboprop and turbofan.

At the top end of the market, Boeing has available a business jet version of the 737 that may be configured in accordance with customers' wishes. The Envoy 7 bizjet version of Dornier's Do728JET regional aircraft is also available. Think of bizjets, however, and the name Lear usually springs to mind. Lear was the market pioneer with its first design (based on a fighter proposed for the Swiss Air Force) in the 1960s. Past products include the

Left: *The ATR 42 ended up carring fifty passengers; the larger ATR 72 can take as many as seventy-four. This is an ATR 72-212 of Simmons Airlines that flies feeder services under American Airlines' American Eagle banner.* Peter R. March

Below Left: *Titan Airways ATR 42-312 G-BUPS. The ATR—Avions de Transport Régional—company was formed by the then Aeritalia and Aerospatiale in 1981. The resultant ATR 42 (originally to carry forty-two passengers) first flew in 1984 and the ATR 42-300, the first production aircraft, the next year. By 2000, sales of this regional airliner were around 350.* Peter R. March

Below: *The Yakovlev Yak-40 tri-jet—NATO reporting name "Codling"—first flew in the 1960s. It was extremely successful, with over 1,000 built when production ceased in the early 1980s.* Peter R. March

23, 24, 25, 28, and 29, and the 35 and 36 models. Acquisition by Bombardier Aerospace in 1990 means that the current model range, which comprises the 31A (with a range of 1,395 miles), 45 (2,0000 miles) and 60 (2,381 miles) is produced under the Bombardier Learjet name. As previously mentioned, Bombardier's expansion in the late 1980s resulted to the acquisition of Canadair, and that company's SE twin-jet, which has a range of 3,120 miles, is now produced under the Bombardier Canadair name. Bombardier Canadair's mid-size

Left: The Boeing Business Jet may open another chapter in the story of its hugely popular 737. The BBJ sees the 737-700 fuselage and the wing (including winglets) and engines of the –800. The prototype is seen at Farnborough in 2000. Peter R. March

Below Left: Originally designed by Canadair, which joined Bombardier in 1986, the Bombardier Challenger can carry up to nineteen passengers. It has sold around 450 of all types, including the latest 604 version seen here landing in Australia. Peter R. March

Below: Another Canadair design, the Bombardier Global Express is a long-range business jet with a distinctive swept wing and winglets. It first flew in 1996 and entered service in 1999. Peter R. March

twin-jet Continental (3,100 miles), Challenger 601 and 604 (3,100 miles), and high-capacity Global Express (6,010 miles) complete the fleet. Rockwell offers both prop and jet models, from the Turbo Commander twin-turboprop to the advanced twin-turbofan Sabreliner.

General aviation giant Cessna has a stake in the market with the Citation family, which has sired some sixteen variants ranging from the first basic Citation I to the long-range, high-speed Citation X. The company also has a range of small capacity turboprop aircraft, including the 404, 411, 401/402, 421, 414, Corsair, Conquest I/II, Caravan II, and T303 Crusader.

Fairchild's acquisition of Swearingen means that their Merlin 23 aircraft is now produced under the Fairchild Dornier name.

One of the newest additions to the bizjet market is Gulfstream Aerospace's G–V. With Bombardier's Global Express, the twin-jet 6,500-mile range G–V is at the very top of the class. Many considered its development to be a folly, but the sales successes have proved that there is a market for an ultra long-

The Aircraft

Above Left: *Raytheon Beech King Air 2000 in Australia.* Peter R. March

Above: *The smaller Bizjet/passenger-carrying market sees many variations on a theme with the biggest manufacturer being Cessna. This is a Cessna Conquest II at Atlanta. Peter R. March*

Left: *Piper PA-42-720 Cheyenne IIIA. Peter R. March*

range business jet. Gulfstream's fleet also includes the Gulfstream IV and VISP. As Grumman Gulfstream, the company built the G159 Gulfstream I, II, and III. Dassault of France considered building an ultra long-range aircraft to complement its fleet but eventually decided against it. Currently in production are the Falcon family of tri-jet aircraft, including the 50, 900B/C/EX, and 2000 models. Raytheon Hawker has the mid-size 800/800XP and 1000 models in its range, together with the Horizon and small-capacity Premier I and Raytheon Beechjet 400.

In the lower capacity (6 to 10 seat) market, the lower running costs of twin and single-engine turboprop models such as Raytheon's King Air models, Pilatus's PC.12, and Piper's Malibu Meridian mean that all have enjoyed good sales.

WALK-AROUND

For the vast majority of the millions of passengers who travel by air every year, the make and model of their transport is of much less importance than the comfort, speed, and safety with which it is able to deliver them to the chosen destination.

Look a little deeper, and in many aspects of its form, the modern airliner bears a superficial resemblance to the aircraft of forty years ago that ushered in the jet age: the de Havilland Comet, the Boeing 707, and Douglas DC-8. In fact, some features can be traced back to the prewar age of air travel, to aircraft such as Boeing's groundbreaking Model 247, which prompted most other passenger aircraft designers to adopt the now familiar low-wing monoplane configuration that has formed the basis of almost every successful airliner since. By the time of the Comet, designers had also adopted the swept wing and tricycle undercarriage. Since then there have been numerous experiments with the location of the powerplant, and the introduction of the wide-body fuselage greatly increased the potential capacity, but the similarities and lineage are readily apparent.

The similarity may be apparent, but the reasons are, perhaps, not abundantly so. In almost every other field of aviation technology, there have been major advances. The fact is that aircraft designers, or at least those concerned with the design of commerical airliners, are bound by certain constraints, which dictate to a large degree the form of their product. First and foremost is the obvious necessity of creating a working flying machine. The second constraint is financial. The airline operators who represent the market are, on the whole, concerned with making money and, as with any commercial organization, this means maximizing profits and reducing overhead costs. To do this, they must carry passengers across a selected route as cheaply as possible, taking into account all the operating costs while maintaining standards of safety, passenger comfort, and aircraft reliability.

Essentially, the airliner must be a compromise between maximum aerodynamic efficiency and load-carrying capacity, and it must be reliable and cheap to operate. From the manufacturer's point of view, it should be relatively easy to construct and be flexible enough to accommodate future modifications. This has led to the formula universally used

today for larger transport aircraft, in which a slender, pressurized fuselage is carried atop a swept wing and a tricycle undercarriage. Although very much the norm today, such a configuration was not always taken for granted, and research continues on future concepts for air travel, including a commercial blended-wing aircraft with passenger accommodation in the thick-chord wing (Northrop Grumman's B-2 Spirit being a current example of this type of aircraft). The decision to build such a machine has yet to be made.

In its current, more familiar form, passenger seating on the airliner is mounted in forward-facing rows separated by one or more aisles to maximize the use of the available space and ease access for passengers and cabin crew. The bulk of the weight, fuel, and baggage/cargo is carried low, near to the center of gravity, and the aircraft is flown from the front. The low-set swept wing is the product of a desire to ensure the passenger cabin is uninterrupted by wing spars, as well as the need for lifting performance and aerodynamic streamlining. Where exceptionally short takeoff performance is sought, or a rear-loading ramp needs to be incorporated into the design, or there is a need to gain clearance for a propeller, a shoulder-set wing is often used.

If, in its basic aspects, commercial aircraft design has followed a familiar formula over the past sixty years, it has also prompted some interesting debates, most notably the location of the powerplant and tail surfaces. We have seen wing, fin, and fuselage-mounted engines, but note that most of the current production airliners utilize wing-mounted engines. However, where ground clearance is a problem, such as on the smaller regional jets such as the ERJ-145 and Bombardier CRJ, tail-mounted engines are a necessity.

Cockpit

One of the best ways to assess how far flight deck technology has come is to compare the cockpits of a 1960s vintage 707 with an ultramodern Boeing 777. Perhaps the most obvious indicator of change is the adoption of digital flight instrumentation, and the use of liquid crystal display

Right: *The new glass cockpits are exemplified by this view of the cockpit of an Airbus 330. Ergonomically designed, computer screens have taken the place of dials.* Peter R. March

screens to present information generated by computerized avionics systems. Computer processing power has vastly increased in the past ten years, and this has spurred the development of increasingly sophisticated avionics. Perhaps the greatest revolution in the field has been the introduction of digital electrical signaling (fly-by-wire) technology and satellite navigation and communication. Although SATNAV and SATCOM were once the preserve of the military, they are now readily available even to the weekend flier. Finally, two-man operation is increasingly the norm on even the most complex aircraft; the flight engineer, who used to have his own station on the flight deck, has become increasingly obsolete because of the availability of automated engine management systems.

The cockpit is the nerve center from where the aircraft is flown, and most of the great multitude of switchgear and monitoring equipment needed for its systems is located there. A modern aircraft has as many as eleven separate systems, namely the flight instrument system, communications, wing configuration (which includes flaps, slats, spoilers, and airbrakes), gear/braking, electrics, hydraulics, environmental control, fire, doors/emergency, fuel, and the engine/auxiliary power unit.

It is perhaps rather difficult to describe the "typical" cockpit, as each is unique to the design of the aircraft and they vary greatly according to the age, size, and function of the aircraft. The flight deck of a four-engine Boeing 747-400 is clearly a rather more complex affair than that of a twin-prop regional transport. With that in mind, basic key equipment will be described, with a focus on a description of the modern glass cockpit, using the Airbus A320 as a model.

The flight deck environment may have changed in form, but not in location. Virtually all commercial transport aircraft are flown from the front by two pilots in side-by-side seating, an arrangement designed to ease crew communications. Aircraft designers have become much more aware of the need for good cockpit ergonomics to reduce stress on the pilots and nowadays they try, so far as is possible, to locate frequently-used controls and equipment within easy reach.

Flying controls

All fixed-wing aircraft have the same basic flying controls for control in three axes—pitch, bank, and yaw. Traditionally, commercial aircraft have been equipped with a floor or panel-mounted control yoke, aileron movement being initiated by rotating

the wheel atop the yoke. Boeing aircraft are standardly equipped with floor-mounted wheel-type control columns (developed by U.S. general aircraft manufacturers in the 1930s to encourage car owners to learn how to fly!), but Airbus has adopted a sidestick type control for its fleet (also used on the F-16 fighter), in which movement of the aileron and elevator control surfaces is initiated by deflecting a small joystick around a base pivot mounted at an ergonomically suitable position on the side of the cockpit. The system has proved popular with pilots, who report that it provides more space in the cockpit. In the 1980s Airbus introduced "fly-by-wire," a term coined for the digital-electrical signaling system it pioneered for the current generation of commercial airliners. A fly-by-wire control system uses electrical circuitry to transmit command inputs from the pilot's yoke or sidestick to the flying surfaces.

Avionics

A modern glass cockpit is based around a suite of avionics equipment, including the central flight management computer (FMC), the electronic flight instrument system (EFIS), and engine indicating and crew alerting system (EICAS). Information from these and other avionics equipment is displayed on multi-function display units (MFDUs). The number of these varies from four to six, and they are used in conjunction with conventional dials on certain aircraft.

Flying instruments

Certain features are common to all transport aircraft. The basic flying instruments are mounted on a panel in front of the pilots' seats, and may be electronically reproduced by the EFIS on the screen of an MFDU, the part of a modern avionics suite known as the primary flight display (PFD), or of the older analog dial type.

These instruments include the altimeter, measuring vertical height above sea level; the vertical speed indicator; airspeed indicator in knots and Mach (with limit values); attitude indicator showing cur-

rent and angles of roll, bank, and yaw (and limit values). An EFIS is able to display additional information, including the location of ground-based navigation aids, data from the FMC, and information from the stall-warning system.

Next to the flying instruments are located the navigation instruments. Again these may be reproduced electronically on an MFDU referred to as the captain's (left) or first officer's (right) navigation display. Navigation instrumentation includes the compasses, the VOR location equipment, chronometer, weather radar, flight path indicator, and (digital) distance and radio magnetic indicator. In an older cockpit such as that found in the 727, the weather radar was mounted on the center console, but with modern MFDU-based systems it is a function of the navigation display. The ND also indicates the position of VOR/DME navaids, ILS marker beacons, waypoint information, estimated time of arrival, distance to go, track to go, and selected runway information. Most aircraft also have a reserve set of dial-type basic flying instruments, mounted on the center panel next to the engine instruments.

Center panel

On the center panel is located the pilot's engine monitoring equipment, including the instruments measuring engine pressure ratios and speeds, intake and exhaust gas temperatures; oil quantity, temperature and pressure; and fuel quantities (used and remaining) and flow rate. Each engine has its own instrumentation, which are displayed in vertical rows to allow for easy cross-reference.

A glass cockpit is typically based around six MFDUs, four of which are used by the EFIS. The other two, known as the primary and secondary engine display, can be configured to display information from the engine management system, and an EICAS (see below).

Center console

Between the two pilots' positions is a center console containing the throttle quadrants, trim wheels, and the prominent wing configuration and gear/engine braking controls. Also found here are the keypads and display screens for the communications equipment, and, if so equipped, the FMC. The FMC lies at the heart of the modern avionics suite, a power-

Left and Above Left: *The old and the new: the difference between the dials of the A300 (above left) and the computers of the A321 are shown well here. On the A321, as with every modern airliner, the "glass" environment has six MFDUs.* Brian A. Strickland, Peter R. March

ful processing system that is used by the crew to automatically navigate the journey (see Chapter 5). The FMC follows a preprogrammed flight plan, which includes the various navigation waypoints and other data such as the fuel load, and is linked to the FCU.

Glareshield/side panels

Depending on the equipment fit, the aircraft may also have various equipment mounted on the instrument panel running along the top of the glareshield, including the flight control unit/mode control. On the A310, the FCU separates the two EFIS control panels (captain/first officer). At the sides of the EFIS control panels are additional panels containing warning lights and chronometer controls.

The FCU panel is used during the flight itself to make short-term adjustments to the preprogrammed FMC system, such as when the crew wishes to make an adjustment to heading or leveling off at an altitude.

Overhead panel

Over the pilots' heads is mounted the panel containing the switchgear to arm and operate the electrical, hydraulic, environmental control, fire, doors, and emergency systems, prominently marked to avoid accidental deployment.

Flight engineer's position

Many large aircraft, such as first-generation 747s, MD-11s, Tristars, and A300s, are equipped with a separate position for a flight engineer, who is responsible for engine monitoring and fuel flow control. His instruments are mounted on a panel on the side of the flight deck.

Above Left: *The uncluttered flight deck of an Aer Lingus Airbus A330 at 37,000 feet over the Atlantic. Note aircraft name (Saint Flannan) on center panel, identifying this as Airbus A330-301 EI-SHN which entered service with the Republic's flag-carrier in the mid-1990s.* Peter R. March

Left: *The big jets often had a station for a third flight deck crew member, the engineer. This is the flight engineer's position on a 747.* Peter R. March

Right: *Compare the spacious cockpit of the A330 long-range airliner with the more cramped arrangement of a long-range business jet. This is a Gulfstream V flight deck as seen at Farnborough in 1997. While the Gulfstream deck may be smaller, it has to be well designed because of the aircraft's remarkable range of over 7,000 miles.* Peter R. March

Navigation

This is one area of aviation technology in which great advances have been made. Although commercial aircraft are still fitted as standard with gyro-stabilized and digital compasses, automatic direction finder (ADF), very high frequency omnirange (VOR), and Digital Distance and Radio Magnetic Indicator (DDRMI) equipment, most are now also equipped with global positioning system (GPS) avionics, slaved to a "moving map" display. GPS avionics use data from the global navigation satellite system (GNSS) operated by the U.S. military to provide accurate (±10m) positional information. The development and commercial availability of GPS technology has undoubtedly given an added boost to aviation safety.

Communications

Satellite technology has also been utilized for global communications networks, including those used to

control the movements of aircraft. Primary ground/air communications are still via UHF/VHF radio equipment. Unfortunately, VHF is limited to line-of-sight communications, and although UHF may work over thousands of miles, at extreme ranges there is a very real degradation in the quality of the signal as the radio waves bounce through the atmosphere. This is obviously something of a problem for airlines who wish to communicate with an aircraft in transoceanic flight. The aircraft communication addressing and reporting system (ACARS), a digital data system based on a network of 600 ground-based waystations and the International Maritime Satellite (INMARSAT) system, and controlled from Maryland, is currently the primary means of overcoming this problem. Another ground/air communication tool is

Left and Below Left: Flightdeck of a BAe 146 landing at Filton in 1993. Peter R. March

Below: Another modern cockpit; this one is of an Aer Lingus Fokker 50 on descent into Dublin. Peter R. March

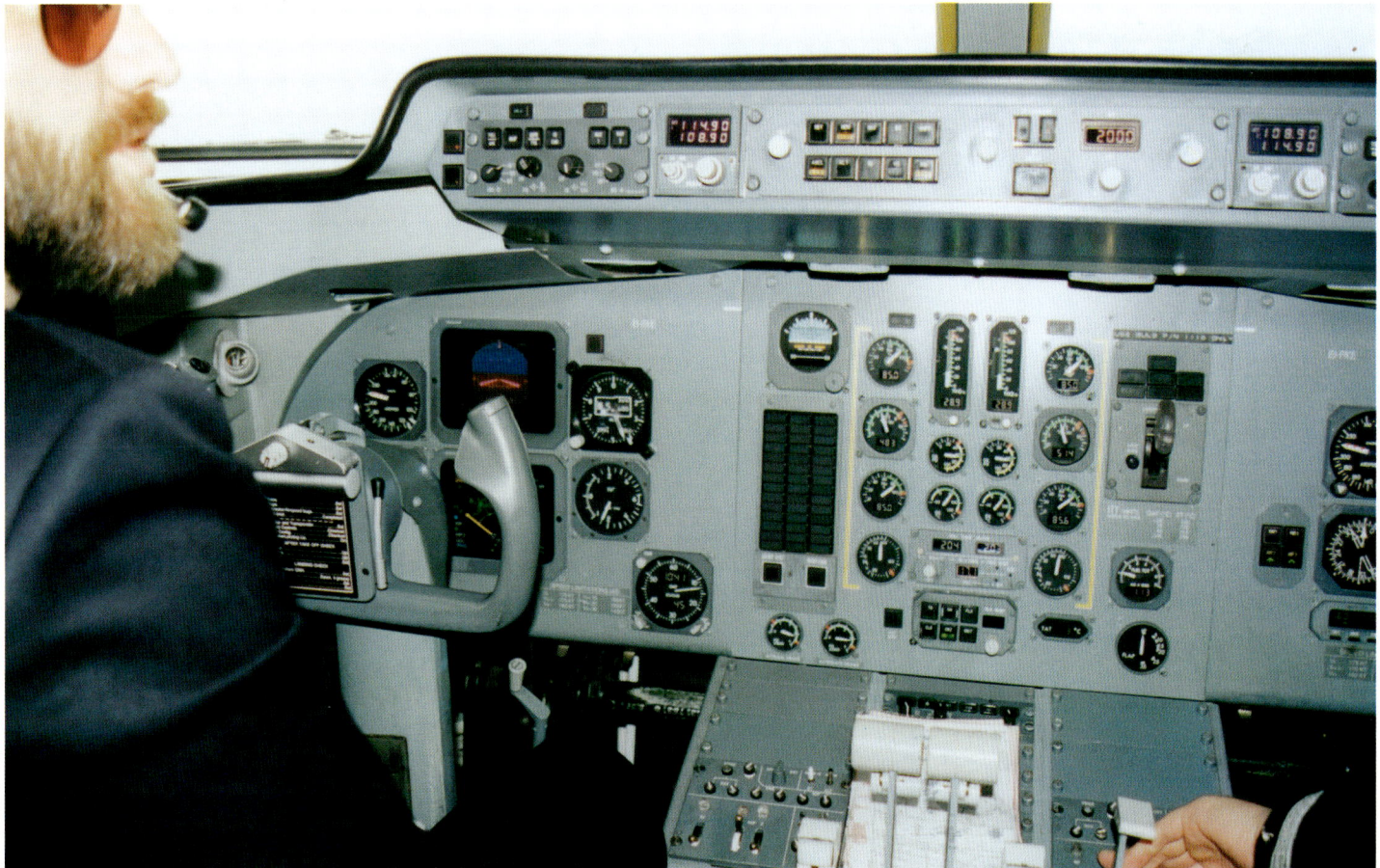

SELCAL, an abbreviation for selective calling, which is also in widespread usage with airlines that operate in remote and oceanic airspace not controlled by radar. Each SELCAL installation has a unique four-letter code, which, should the operator or ATC wish to communicate with the aircraft, is transmitted as an audio signal. The onboard decoder recognizes this sound and alerts the crew, establishing voice contact via radio (thereby dispensing with the need to monitor the UHF frequency). However, there is no auto-tune, as with the ACARS, and the equipment must be tuned to one of three specific frequencies during the flight.

Wings and flaps

The primary lifting surface on a fixed-wing aircraft is its wing, which generates lift; simply put, when the pressure of the air flowing over the wing is less than that on the lower surface. Forward motion through the air is required to generate lift; for level flight the lift produced must be equal to the weight of the aircraft and at takeoff or during the climbing phase, greater than the weight of the aircraft. Aerodynamics is, of course, a more complex science

The Aircraft

than this, and the design of the optimum wing profile is an exacting process, but for our purposes, it will suffice.

The location and design of the wing varies greatly; where STOL performance is more important, a mildly swept, high-set wing may be used; where high cruising speed is sought, a thinner, more steeply swept low-set wing is best. Inevitably a compromise between high-speed efficiency and low-speed lifting ability is sought. With as large and as heavy a machine as a commercial airliner, the wing cannot generate sufficient lift at certain angles of attack (such as during takeoff and landing) without additional lifting surfaces. Most important of these are the flaps, mounted on both the leading and the trailing edges of the wing inboard of the ailerons. These are powered by screw-type hydraulic jacks and controlled by levers mounted on the center console, and when deployed they track outward and down and change the profile of the wing, helping to

Wings come in all shapes and sizes as these three photos show. The high position—shown on the Shorts 360 Titan (Above Left)—is often used for smaller aircraft that operate in short landing and takeoff environments. The lower, more aerodynamic approach is shown with the de Havilland Dove (Below) and the amazing Beech Starship 1 (Left). All: Peter R. March

generate lift at takeoff and landing. There are a number of different systems, such as the Zaparka, Fowler, Krueger, and blown flap. The heavier 747 has full-span leading-edge Krueger flaps and massive, triple-slotted trailing-edge flaps to help it generate lift. A smaller aircraft such as the 737 has a rather less complex system of leading-edge Krueger flaps and slotted trailing-edge flaps. Various degrees of flap can be set. Links into various alarm systems warn of incorrect wing configuration, which could be disastrous in certain situations. Another lift

device is the leading-edge slat, which acts in a way something like a jib ahead of the mainsail on a sailing boat.

Landing gear

That small puff of smoke thrown up at the point when an airliner touches down gives an indication of the punishment endured by the gear and braking systems. At the same time, they must be faultlessly reliable. The tricycle-type undercarriage system now universally used keeps the aircraft on an even keel and replaced the taildragger type system of the 1940s.

Low-speed steering, another function of the gear/braking system, is via the nose gear, which is controlled by hydraulic actuators slaved to the rudder pedals or else to a cockpit-mounted tiller wheel. When a certain speed is attained, steering switches to the rudder.

The nose gear of a modern airliner is an oleo-pneumatic (oil-using) strut typically carrying a

Left: The thin, slightly swept wing and trailing-edge flaps of an Airbus A321 of Air Inter are shown off perfectly in this photograph taken at a Moscow airshow. Peter R. March

Below and Below Left: Two views of undersides showing different trailing-edge flap configurations. The size of the aircraft's wing obviously has a bearing on the flap arrangement: note the three strakes on the Cathay Pacific Airbus A340 (Below Left), as against the two on the Virgin Boeing 737-300 (Below). Both: Peter R. March

twin-wheel bogie; the main gear legs carry two (737) to six (777) wheel bogies. The 747 has the largest number of wheels of any commercial aircraft, with a two-wheel nose gear and four main gear legs each mounting a four wheel bogie.

The wheels are retracted into the undercarriage bays using hydraulic jacks. The cockpit actuator is usually a fairly simple affair, indicating "up" or "down." There are instrument warning lights to show both these positions as "locked." Because of the great drag of the lowered undercarriage, there are strict limits as to when it may be safely deployed. In the event of a systems malfunction the gear can usually be wound down manually.

The tires on aircraft are manufactured using a steel-wire carcass and a high-density rubber compound, and are deeply grooved around their circumference to aid cooling of the surface and water dispersion.

On the wheel axles are vented discs and hydraulic braking calipers, which are controlled by a footbrake in the footwell in the cockpit. This is used for low-speed taxiing, and may in turn be slaved to a master computerized control system that operates both the wheel and engine braking systems automatically during the landing run.

Engine braking is dealt with below. Air braking is achieved by disrupting the airflow over the surface of the wing and increasing drag. On commercial aircraft, spoilers are mounted on the upper wing surfaces and on command extend at right angles to the wing, enabling the pilot to kill some of his forward speed during an excessively fast approach or when descending at a steep angle.

Left: *The undercarriage of a Fairchild Aerospace Do328/JET begins to deploy from its hull recesses. (Compare this jet version of the Do328 with the turboprop 328-110 on page 48.)* Daniel J. March

Below and Below Left: *Landing gear also comes in a wide range of sizes, locations and arrangements depending on the size and operating environments of the aircraft concerned. These two high-tail, rear-engined Bombardier regional jets—the Global Express and Challenger 604 (Below)—show typical tricycle landing gear. Note the puff of smoke from the Global Express's gear.* Both: Peter R. March

The Aircraft

Three more views of undercarriage deployment, showing an HS125-400 (Above Left), an MD-82 of Scandinavian (Above) and the amazing SATIC A300-600ST Beluga (Left). The latter is the widest-ever civil jet and carries Airbus components to their final assembly points at Toulouse and Hamburg. All: Peter R. March

Electrics

Modern fly-by-wire digital technology, in-flight entertainment systems, and complex avionics have greatly increased the complexity of aircraft electrical systems, and today the electrical system is perhaps the most complex part of the aircraft. During construction, its installation requires a considerable number of man-hours—the Boeing 747-400, for example, has over 135 miles of cabling, and its electrical generators produce 14kVA. The 777, by contrast, needs nearly three times that amount. The electricity for the aircraft is provided by engine-driven generators, and sometimes also by the tail-mounted APU. Because of the reliance on electrical power, multiple redundancy is built into the system, and automatic regulation ensures that in the event of partial power loss (due to an engine shut-down), vital systems are prioritized. The master switch gear for the electrical systems is contained on the overhead panel.

Hydraulics

Hydraulic power is used to operate a multitude of aircraft functions, such as lowering and raising the undercarriage, operating the wheel brakes and flying surfaces, and changing wing configuration. It is generated by engine-driven units and, in the event of an emergency, may be provided by a drop-down ram-air turbine. Again, multiple redundancy is built into the system, each aircraft having as many as three independent systems each capable of generating sufficient power for the aircraft to be controlled in the event of loss of the other(s).

Environmental Control System

The pressure, purity, and temperature of the air inside the aircraft is controlled by the ECS, via the master switch gear on the overhead panel in the cockpit. The air on a passenger aircraft is maintained at a slightly lower pressure than atmospheric air, and is also much cleaner. Passengers often experience a light-headedness, coupled with swelling of hands, feet, and stomach as a result, and there is the

Below: Qantas Boeing 767-338ER showing off the larger undercarriage assembly required for one of the big jets. Peter R. March

suggestion of a link between this and other cardio-vascular problems (such as deep vein thrombosis).

Carbon dioxide and other impurities are removed by filtering and fresh oxygen is generated by chemical means. Temperature is controlled by heat diffusers which are cooled by atmospheric air. Pressurized air is ducted around the aircraft via pipes and nozzles at strategic points in the cabin and above the seating positions, which provide for some degree of passenger control.

EMERGENCIES

It is hoped, of course, that the emergency systems will never have to be used. Reducing the threat of an emergency situation is the task of the crew, the maintenance staff, and the air traffic controllers. In the air, where the threat is greatest, the crew has various avionics systems to help them.

Fire

Fire is obviously a major threat to an aircraft brimming with hundreds of thousands of pounds of aviation fuel. Detection and suppression of the threat is the function of the fire control system, monitored and controlled by master warning lights

on the instrument panels and switchgear on the overhead panel.

A network of sensors in the baggage hold, passenger cabin, wheel bays, and surrounding the engines is linked to the master warning system, and in the event of a fire, this alerts the crew with both audible and visual alarms. Remote fire suppression is achieved by the application of chemical supressants through strategically mounted nozzles; smaller fires in the cabin, perhaps ignited by an illicit cigarette in the toilet waste bin, may be tackled by the cabin crew using hand-held equipment.

Emergency doors

An airliner has both normal cabin doors and emergency exit doors. The doors form an interference (plug) fit with the fuselage structure. The normal boarding and cargo-loading doors are hinged and the emergency doors are removable. Some aircraft, notably the corporate business jets, have a folding stair which can be retracted into the cabin.

Emergency doors are located over the wings, and the boarding doors located along the cabin, or in some cases under the rear fuselage. The doors can be locked either manually or remotely from the cockpit. Despite seeming complex, the mechanisms are necessarily simple to allow for easy operation under emergency conditions. Cargo doors must be sufficiently large so as to allow for loading industry standard cargo pallets, yet at the same time not compromise the structural integrity of the aircraft.

The cabin doors are also equipped with self-inflating slides, which can be deployed both manually from the cabin and remotely from the cockpit. In an emergency, these allow passengers to exit the aircraft quickly.

Emergency lighting for low-light conditions (perhaps as a result of smoke) is situated along the aisles and at the exit points, and is powered by independent power reserves. It will be triggered automatically when the door slides deploy. Emergency oxygen masks, consisting of a simple mouthpiece, head restraint, and supply tube, are fitted above each passenger seat and crew seating position. Should the aircraft suffer sudden decompression or loss of height, these will drop down and the air supply will automatically engage. Both of these systems are armed, and may be manually deployed from the overhead panel.

Stall warning system

Designed to provide advance warning to the pilot of the onset of a stall, stall warning systems can provide aural and visual alerts and may also incorporate a "stick-pusher" which automatically forces the control column forward if the aircraft is entering a stall.

Ground proximity warning system

As its name suggests, this warns the pilot if he is too close to the ground, and in such a situation an audible warning sounds in the cockpit which urges the pilot to "pull-up, pull-up." The original GPWS was developed in the early 1970s, and uses radio waves to monitor the ground directly beneath the aircraft. However, it is unable to detect obstructions ahead.

Left and Overleaf: *When it all goes wrong in the air, those on the ground need to do everything possible to ensure the safety of the passengers. All airports have extensive fleets of emergency vehicles such as the fire tender seen here at Birmingham International Airport and the fire trucks and firefighters at Bournemouth International Airport (Overleaf).* Brian A. Strickland, Andrew March, Peter R. March

71

The Aircraft

An advanced system, which has been standard equipment on all Boeing aircraft since 1998, uses a database containing data on the geographical configuration, GPS, and cockpit displays (information can be displayed on the Navigation Display) to provide advance warning of potential hazards. The U.S. government has made it mandatory for passenger aircraft to carry the equipment, and other authorities are following suit.

Traffic collision avoidance system
TCAS and derivative systems will assume steadily increasing importance in coming years as the volume of air traffic rises. TCAS warns of other aircraft in close proximity, advises of their heading, height, and speed, and gives advice as to emergency avoidance measures.

Flight data recorder
During the course of the flight, the FDR routinely records aircraft and engine performance (height, heading, speed, EPR, and more), which may later be used to analyze the events leading up to a crash. The famous "black box" is actually orange (to aid searchers), and is designed to withstand a high impact. The data is recorded on wire.

Cockpit voice recorder
In-flight communications between the crew are recorded by this device, which can provide additional information to crash investigators. However, CVRs may not used by the company to spy on their pilots.

ENGINES
When taking stock of the revolution in civil aviation that has occurred in the past fifty years, it is difficult to find any more important catalyst than the introduction of the jet engine. Pioneered in Britain, developed both there and in Germany during World War II, and thereafter the focus of intensive research and development in the United States, Europe, and the Soviet Union, jet propulsion opened the door to longer, faster commercial flying. The early jetliners

Below: *Cockpit of a Boeing 747-200 belonging to Northwest standing at Gatwick.* Peter R. March

The Aircraft

were comparatively crude, noisy and dirty, but progressive development over the past sixty years has improved immeasurably the efficiency and reliability (and equally the complexity) of the jet engine. Under increasing pressure from environmental groups and the demands of operators whose dramatically increased fuel costs are threatening profitability, engine manufacturers are seeking further ways of increasing efficiency by reducing emissions, consumption, and noise.

Before we examine in more detail the current market in aircraft engines, let us look first at what actually provides the motive force. A propulsion system actually consists of two component parts—first, the fuel, which is the energy source from which propulsive force is produced; and second, the engine, which is a mechanical device by which the energy of the fuel is transferred into propulsive force. With aircraft, the propulsive force is provided by accelerating a gas rearward, which for conventional aircraft is the air through which the aircraft is passing. Within this category, aircraft propulsion systems may be divided into two classes, those in which the rearward acceleration of the gas (air) is caused by the rotation of a propeller; and those in which the acceleration takes place in the engine itself.

Either system must meet three basic requirements. First, and paramount, is low weight; second is reliability; and third, low cost (including both unit cost and operating costs). Low noise is also becoming a fundamental requirement in the wake of stringent new noise regulations at many European airports.

Weight

It is obviously also desirable to build as light an engine as possible, or more accurately, one that will be a sufficiently low percentage of the gross weight of the aircraft (airframe, propulsion system, and payload). In addition, the weight of the propulsion system must be divided so that a useful quantity of fuel can be carried.

Above Left and Left: *Airport services have to cater for a wide range of engine types from old props—as exemplified by this DH Heron of Jersey Airlines to the modern turbofans of this modern Learjet 60 (Left) at Alicante.* Both: Peter R. March

Selecting a suitable propulsion system has been one of the fundamental tasks of aircraft design since the earliest days of powered flight and requires detailed and careful analysis and deliberation. The lack of suitably light and powerful propulsion systems, more than any other factor, governed the progress of aviation during the late twentieth century. The best of the current generation of turbofans produce over four times the thrust per pound of the weight of the engine. Before selecting a suitable engine—or issuing a requirement for one, should none currently exist—the aircraft design team considers carefully their thrust ratio requirements and must also take into consideration the fact that thrust varies according to speed and altitude.

Having determined the weight of the engine, the remaining proportion of the weight allocated to the propulsion system is used for fuel. The range of the aircraft is determined by the energy content of the fuel and the efficiency with which this energy is transformed into thrust. The fuel used by commercial airlines is a high-grade petroleum, with a relatively high energy content, and this energy is converted by the engine into thrust by burning the fuel in air passed through the engine. Engine efficiency depends on the type, speed, and altitude, and varies from around ten to sixty percent. A perfectly efficient engine (100 percent) would convert one pound of petroleum into one pound of thrust for a distance of 3,000 miles. In practical terms, one pound of aviation fuel burned in an engine produces one pound of thrust for 300 to 1,800 miles.

Together, these three factors—specific weight of the engine, its efficiency, and the heat energy of the fuel—determine the suitability of the propulsion system for the aircraft and for the flight mission it has to perform.

Reliability

The second major requirement of the propulsion system is that it is reliable. Reliability can be increased by using more than one engine—providing the aircraft is able to fly on less than all the engines—but this in turn increases the likelihood of engine failure and the overall complexity of the propulsion system. During the 1950s and 1960s, there was much debate over the preferred number of engines on a commercial transport aircraft. For long-distance overwater operations, four engines

75

were considered a must, and the family of 1960s tri-jets were born out of a similar desire for acceptable levels of safety.

However, in the past twenty years engine reliability has increased immeasurably, and has permitted the redrafting of the rules governing prolonged overwater operations for aircraft equipped with certain engines with proven reliability. Combined with increased efficiency, this has allowed for a reduction in the number of engines on modern designs, and flights that would previously have been permissible only with three or more engines are now possible with twin-jets. Correspondingly, the manufacturers are making aircraft to fit the new requirements. At the current time, the twin-jet predominates in the civil aviation market. Only one of the current Boeing offerings (B747) and a single Airbus family (A340) has more than two engines, and the former is a thirty-year-old design. Furthermore, the company has serious doubts that another four-engine high capacity airliner is needed, whereas Airbus has committed to one in the form of the A380.

Increased reliability has also helped to increase service intervals, partly offsetting the dramatic rise in fuel prices since the early 1970s, while advanced engine and fuel management systems have reduced pilot workload and heralded the decline in the flight engineer's role. Reliability is generally determined by the length of time that an engine can run without need for a major overhaul and by the frequency of minor failures. This varies according to the use to which the aircraft is put because of the greater stresses placed on it under certain conditions, such as during takeoff.

Before it is certified by the FAA/CAA (and more recently under the European Joint Aviation Regulations), a new aircraft is tested extensively "on the stand" to determine the parameters of its performance. To replicate conditions during a flight cycle, the test runs include periods of acceleration, full-throttle, partial throttle, and idling. On completion of this trial, the engine is certified at various ratings, stating duration for which it may be operated at each setting.

Types of propulsion systems

As previously mentioned, aircraft propulsion systems can be divided according to the means used to produce thrust into propeller engines and jet engines. They can be divided again according to the type of fuel used, into air-breathing and rocket engines, and yet further into external and internal-combustion engines. Chemically-powered internal-combustion engines have predominated in the field of powered flight. In the field of commerical aviation two types are used, the reciprocating engine and the turbine engine (which includes the turbojet, turboshaft, turboprop, and turbofan). Reciprocating engines are still common in general aviation and for light transport aircraft, but they have long since been abandoned by designers of large commerical aircraft in favor of the turbine.

Turbine engines differ from reciprocating engines (the workings of which are not described here) by way of the fact that the cooling air is passed through rather than around the outside of the engine, along with the combustion air.

Turboprop engines were introduced in England (Vickers Viscount) and Europe in 1953 and in the U.S. in 1956. They are widely used, particularly on commuter and business aircraft, and on a range of military and civil heavy lifters, and in applications where their rapid acceleration and braking abilities are useful. Although lighter and more powerful by weight than a reciprocating engine, the turboprop is limited to speeds of around 550 mph and altitudes of 40,000 feet. Above this speed, efficient and sufficiently light propellers have yet to be developed.

The turbine engine is, to a certain extent, free of these limitations. Instead of expanding the hot gases through the turbine stages required to drive a propeller, these stages can be eliminated and the expansion of gases can take place through a nozzle discharging directly rearward of the aircraft. This creates the thrust that is the propulsive force of the aircraft. This type of engine, termed the turbojet, made high speed and even supersonic flight a practical reality. It was simpler to develop

Above Left: A Tupolev Tu154B-2 of Malev Hungarian Airlines. Like the Boeing 727, DC-10 and Tristar, the Tu154 has a tri-jet arrangement. Peter R. March

Left: The Fairchild-Dornier 728JET is a 70-seat development of the Do328. Powered by General Electric CF34 engines, it is due to enter service in 2003. Peter R. March

than the more mechanically complex turboprop (which has reduction gearboxes), was introduced earlier, and powered the first generation of jet aircraft, including the commercial jetliners of the early 1950s. The first turbojets were noisy, smoky, and not particularly fuel-efficient and engine manufacturers sought ways to improve them, resulting in the modern turbofan engine. Since they were introduced by Rolls-Royce and Pratt & Whitney in the late 1950s, turbofans have increased in size, complexity, efficiency, and power. It would require rather more space than is afforded here to describe in detail the workings of one of these machines, so this description is necessarily brief.

A turbine engine consists of inlet, compressor, burner, turbine, and nozzle. The inlet functions to capture and decelerate air prior to entry into the compressor. While the inlet is often optimized for cruising conditions, it must provide adequate mass-flow during all other engine operating conditions including takeoff, maneuvering, and landing. At the subsonic speed ranges in which airliners operate, the ideal inlet is a "pod" or "pitot" installation, as seen on most modern jetliners, which makes full use of the ram effect and has minimum size, weight, and effect on the aircraft's aerodynamics. There have been a number of experiments with alternative pod installations, notably the de Havilland Comet and Tupolev Tu-104 which had quad engines buried in the wing roots, and the trunk type installation seen on the supersonic BAC/ Aerospatiale Concorde.

The compressor functions to increase the pressure of the air entering the engine, optimizing the conditions for combustion and expansion of the air downstream. It consists of a moving impeller and a stationary diffuser. The axial type compressor has replaced the centrifugal type compressor that was a feature of the first generation of jet engines. Axial compressors can accommodate more airflow and

are more efficient at producing thrust, but individually cannot provide enough compression for an aircraft powerplant, and for this reason as many as fifteen separate high, intemediate, and low-pressure compression stages are used on modern high bypass ratio turbofan engines to produce a sufficient volume of pressurized air.

Pressurized airflow passes from the compressor into the burner. In order to assure ignition, the mixture of fuel and air must be correctly proportioned and of relatively low velocity. However, far more air passes through the engine than is required for the complete combustion of the fuel, so the burner parcels out a small portion of the air for combustion and decelerates it in the "primary" zone. The gases that are the product of combustion are hotter than any current technology turbine is capable of tolerating and so the remaining air is remixed with the hot gases to produce a nearly uniform temperature stream entering the turbine. A modern high bypass ratio turbofan uses a totally annular burner, the flame tube forming a ring around the entire engine, which is a major improvement upon the earlier "can" and "can-annular" type burners.

Downstream of the combuster, the turbine provides the torque that is necessary to drive the compressor and any other auxiliary equipment. Turbines are also used to drive fans (turbofan), rotors (turboshaft), and propellers (turboprop). Turbines operate in an extreme environment and are made of some of the most advanced materials yet devised. Even using these materials, the turbine inlet temperature is limited by the strength of the blade materials, and since inlet temperature has a governing effect on engine performance, there is a great desire to operate at temperatures near to the limits of the material. For this reason, advanced blade cooling schemes are employed. The turbine actually works like a compressor in reverse; a series of static nozzles converts pressure to velocity, and the moving section converts that velocity to rotational motion. Much more extreme blade angles are possible, as the turbine is moving pressure rather than adding it, and a turbine generally has far fewer stages than a compressor. However, the stresses are much higher, due to higher temperatures, greater blade angles, and centrifugal forces.

The nozzle serves to convert any energy remaining in the flow (after the turbine) into kinetic

Above Left: Still a class act, the Cessna 650 Citation first flew in the late 1970s. A twin-engined business jet aimed at the high end of the market, it could carry six to nine passengers. Peter R. March

Left: The Boeing 777 could be powered by Rolls-Royce Trent, P&W PW4074, or GE90 turbofans. Here, one of Thai Airways International's first 777s—powered by Trents—comes in to land at Kai Tak, Hong Kong, with the distinctive Lion Rock in the background. Peter R. March

energy by decreasing the pressure and accelerating the flow. This results in thrust. Nozzle design is vital because to a large degree it determines the turbine entry temperature and therefore the turbine efficiency, the mass flow of the engine, the exit velocity and exit pressure, all of which determine thrust. It must take into account the behavior of the air and potential losses resulting from friction, and also the high temperatures and pressure of the efflux.

Modern airliner engines use high bypass turbofan engines, in which a turbine engine drives another system—a large front-mounted fan which provides as much as seventy-five percent of the thrust to propel the aircraft. The engine is contained within a large bypass air duct through which the bypass air travels before it exits at the rear.

The turboprop bears a functional similarity to the turbofan, in that the shaft of the engine is used to drive another system. The other system is in this case a gearbox and a propeller, rather than a ducted fan. The core engine is designed with more focus on creating torque, rather than providing thrust. The core usually accounts for less than ten percent of the total thrust of the engine.

The last of the group of turbine-driven engines which have aeronautical applications is the turboshaft, similar in concept to the turboprop, but instead of the propeller, the shaft exits to some other device, commonly a helicopter rotor.

Thrust Reversing

Although most aircraft brakes are sufficient during normal conditions, thrust reversing provides an additional means of bringing the aircraft to a halt during its ground run, which is obviously advantageous in icy or wet conditions, or when the pilot wishes to minimize his taxiing time to the stand. High bypass ratio turbofan engines reverse thrust by changing the direction of the fan airflow,

Above Left: Scandinavian MD-87 powered by two Pratt & Whitney turbofans seen at Moscow. Peter R. March

Left: Engines, like aircraft, come in different sizes, and make different amounts of noise. The four Textron Lycoming ALF502 turbofans that powered the BAe146 were renowned for their low noise levels. The 146 regional jet was designed for shorter ranges into smaller fields where performance and noise levels were critical. Peter R. March

and turboprop aircraft reverse the thrust by changing the pitch of the propeller. Usually a hydro-mechanical system is used to change the blade angle, giving a braking response when activated. There are a number of different systems; the first utilizes clam-shell type deflector doors to reverse the exhaust gas stream; the second uses target type deflector doors for the same purpose; and the third (used on fan engines) utilizes blocker doors to reverse the cold (bypass) airflow. The first two systems are pneumatically and hydraulically actuated, and act to deflect the hot exhaust gases forward (at an angle of about forty-five degrees). The cold stream reverse system is actuated by an air motor, the output of which is converted to mechanical movement by flexible drives, gearboxes, and screw jacks. During normal operation, the reverse thrust cascade vanes are covered by the blocker doors. On selection of reverse thrust, the actuation system folders the blocker doors to blank off the cold airstream final nozzle, thus diverting the airflow through the cascade vanes.

Noise suppression

This has become one of the most important fields of research due to the increasingly strict regulations imposed by airports and aircraft noise certification requirements. These govern the maximum noise level aircraft are allowed to produce. Although airframe generated noise is a factor in an aircraft's overall noise signature, the principal source of noise is the powerplant.

Engine noise emanates from the fan, compressor, turbine, and exhaust jets. Turbulence in the exhaust stream and "sonic boom" generated when the efflux exceeds the speed of sound are the principal sources of this noise, and means to reduce both are the main areas of research. One technique is to induce a rapid or shorter mixing region to reduce low and high-frequency noise. This is achieved by increasing the contact area between the exhaust gas stream and the atmosphere by using a nozzle incorporating a corrugated or lobe-type noise suppressor.

In the late 1990s, tough new noise restrictions were imposed in both the U.S. and in Europe, which forced operators of older aircraft to fit "hush kits" to the powerplant. These are basically an extension of the nozzle, making use of complex internal

Above: *Ilyushin Il-62M of Aviaenegro at Moscow's Sheremetievo Airport. The Il-62M first flew in the early 1970s and in spite of improved engine nacelles, is still a noisy aircraft whose Soloviev D-30KU turbofans were designed for a less critical period.* Peter R. March

Right: *The 767 was designed to different criteria. A medium-range airliner, the 767 also became a very long-range airliner when a number of engine combinations gained the ETOPS extended-range approval. This Airtours Boeing 767-31KER is seen landing at Alicante.* Peter R. March

The Aircraft

The Aircraft

acoustics to supress the sound waves. A different interpretation of the regulations in Europe and the U.S. almost prompted a major trade war, as many U.S. operators found themselves disbarred from flights into European airports.

Emissions reduction

Another criticism aimed at air transportation is its contribution to global warming, and its consumption of fossil fuels. A number of environomental groups are in favor of rationing fuel, a move which is strongly opposed by the industry, which favors a more evolutionary approach to the problem through the development of new technologies. Aircraft contribute about three percent of the annual total of greenhouse gases, and less than three percent of the Nox-type gases. Over the past forty years, fuel efficiency per passenger kilometer has improved by seventy percent, and total consumption is predicted to rise more slowly in comparison to the traffic increase.

Manufacturers

The U.S., Europe, and Russia are the main centers of turbine engine production. Although the industry is highly competitive, the enormous cost of developing a new engine has prompted a number of alliances as a risk and cost-sharing strategy.

Described here is most of the current range of turbofan engines. These may be divided into low, medium, and high-thrust categories. At the lower end of the thrust range (0-15,000lb max thrust), aimed predominantly at the regional and business aircraft market, Honeywell offers its ALF502 (7,000lb/BAe146), AS907 (7,900lb/Bombardier Continental), AS977 (7,000lb/BAe Systems RJX),

LF507 (7,000lb/BAe Systems RJ70), and the seven models of the TFE731 family (3,500-5,000lb). Pratt & Whitney Canada offers the three models in the JT15D family (2,500-3,000lb, used on Cessna Citation), four variants of the PW300 (4,600-8,100 lb; Learjet 60, Galaxy Aerospace Galaxy, Dassault Falcon 2000EX), and two PW500 variants (2,700-3,800lb; Cessna Citation Bravo/Excel). Ukrainian manufacturer Ivchenko Progress has the lower thrust range AI-22 (8,400lb; Tupolev Tu-234) and Rolls-Royce supplies four variants of its AE3007 (6,700-8,500lb) turbofan for the Embraer ERJ 135/145, Legacy, EJR-RJ140, and the Cessna Citation. At the lowest end of the thrust range, Williams International of Michigan has engines ranging from the 800lb thrust EJ22 to the 2,300lb FJ44-2 (Sino Swearingen SJ30-2, Cessna Citation CJ2, Raytheon Premier).

The medium-thrust market, encompassing engines within the 15,000-35,000lb range, is now largely the domain of the sole CFM International (a joint company owned by SNECMA of France and General Electric) engine family, the popular and versatile CFM56. Available in six variants ranging from 18,500 to 31,200lb thrust, the more powerful versions feature double annular combusters. They are equipped with Boeing 737–300/400/500, Boeing 767-600/700/800/900 and Business Jet, and Airbus A318/319/320/321 and A340-200/300 models. Its chief rival is the International Aero Engines (Pratt & Whitney, Rolls-Royce, JAEC, and MTU) V2500, which is offered in ten variants ranging from the 22,000lb V2500-A1 to the 33,000lb V2533-A5. Ukrainian manufacturer Aviadgetal produces the 24,200lb D-30 for the Il-62M, Il-76T, and Beriev A-40; Ivchenko Progress the 16,900lb D-436 for the Tupolev Tu-334, Beriev Be-2000 and Yakovlev Yak-42M. Pratt & Whitney's JT8D engine has been in production since the 1960s, and currently it is produced in -15, -17, -200, -209, -217, -217B/C and -219 variants for the Boeing 727, 737, and MD-80/-82/-83/-87/-88. A new offering from the company is the PW6000, a 23,000lb thrust which began flight testing in August 2000 and is targeted at Airbus A318 customers.

The most keenly contested market sector is the higher thrust (35,000lb-plus) bracket, in which GE, Rolls-Royce, and Pratt & Whitney each have major shares. General Electric, which in 2000 purchased

The Aircraft

fellow U.S. manufacturer Honeywell, is engaged in a battle for position over the Airbus A380, with GE offering the proposed 70,000lb GE/P&W GP7270 and Rolls its 75,000lb Trent 900. GE currently has its CF6 engine in production (49,900-69,900lb) for the Airbus A310, A300-600, and A330, as well as the Boeing 747-300/400, 767, and MD-11, and is also developing its GE90 model, which is currently offered for the 777 and rated at 76,900lb. If this development goes according to schedule, the GE90-115B derivative will, at 115,000lb thrust, be the most powerful jet engine ever built, and is aimed at the 777-200LR and 300ER markets.

Pratt & Whitney's position in the market has slipped slightly in recent years, a situation it hopes to correct through the alliance with GE and with the all-new PW6000 engine it is currently testing. In the higher thrust arena, the 45,000 JT9D is no longer produced but commonly seen on Airbus A300-600 and A310 aircraft, on Boeing 747 and 767s, and on Douglas DC-10s. Its PW2000 (38,000-40,000lb thrust) and PW4000 (52,000-84,000lb thrust) engines are the most important revenue earners, and the company has a share in the IAE V2500. It has also announced plans to develop a geared fan engine aimed at the lower thrust bracket.

The other industry giant, Rolls-Royce, has two engines in the higher thrust bracket, the 43,000-60,700lb RB211, which powers Boeing's 747-400 and 757 and the Tupolev Tu-204, and the Trent family, which includes variants of the −500 (56,000lb), -600 (72,000lb), -700 (71,000lb) and −800 and will also include the -900 (75,000lb). Under development is a 104,000lb thrust engine with swept fans. Trent powers Airbus A330-200/300/500, A340-500/600, Boeing 747 and 767, 777-200/200ER/-300, and is proposed (-900) for the A380.

Above Left: United Airlines Boeing 777 seen at Amsterdam's Schipol airport. Peter R. March

Left: Ansett Australia Airbus A320 seen above Melbourne. Ansett started flying in 1936 with a Fokker Universal and is the largest privately-owned airline in Australia. Peter R. March

Auxiliary Power Unit
In addition to its main engines, the airliner is also likely to have an auxiliary engine known as the APU to drive its start-up systems, and to provide backup and emergency power in the event of an engine-out situation. The APU also provides a measure of independence from ground generators, useful for operations at smaller strips.

The APU is usually located toward the rear, at the base of the fin or under the rear empennage. It is controlled and monitored from the cockpit; the switchgear is usually located on the overhead panel.

Engine and Fuel Management
The task of engine management, once the role of the flight engineer, is now being assumed by computers. Many older aircraft still require a flight engineer, but on the new generation of airliners, two-man operation is the norm. The transition caused something of a hiatus in the industry, but when one looks at the hard economics of the situation, it was inevitable that the computer was always going to win. Traditionally, the engine instruments are mounted on the center panel, and with the current glass cockpit technology, Engine Pressure Ratio (EPR) and Exhaust Gas Temperature values and limits are presented on the PED, along with thrust limit, flap position, and fuel flow in pounds per hour. On the SED, fuel used, oil quantity, oil pressure, oil temperature, and engine bleed pressure are displayed and, during start-up, data from the ignitors and start valves. Also shown are vibration levels and fuel and oil filter status. Data from the engine sensors is processed by the EICAS.

Auto-throttles are a more recent innovation, whereby the pilot simply pushes a button mounted on one of the thrust levers prior to commencing the takeoff run. The thrust levers come forward automatically until the takeoff EPR is met. The FMS calculates the rotation speeds and EPRs for the conditions and the pilot is only required to lift the aircraft off the ground, with the autothrottles maintaining the speed, altitude, and climb rate programmed into the autopilot. Currently, the state-of-the-art in engine management is Full Authority Digital Engine Control, which has the capability to optimize engine performance during a normal flight, such as bleed-air extractions, bypass ratios, and gearbox speed ratios.

87

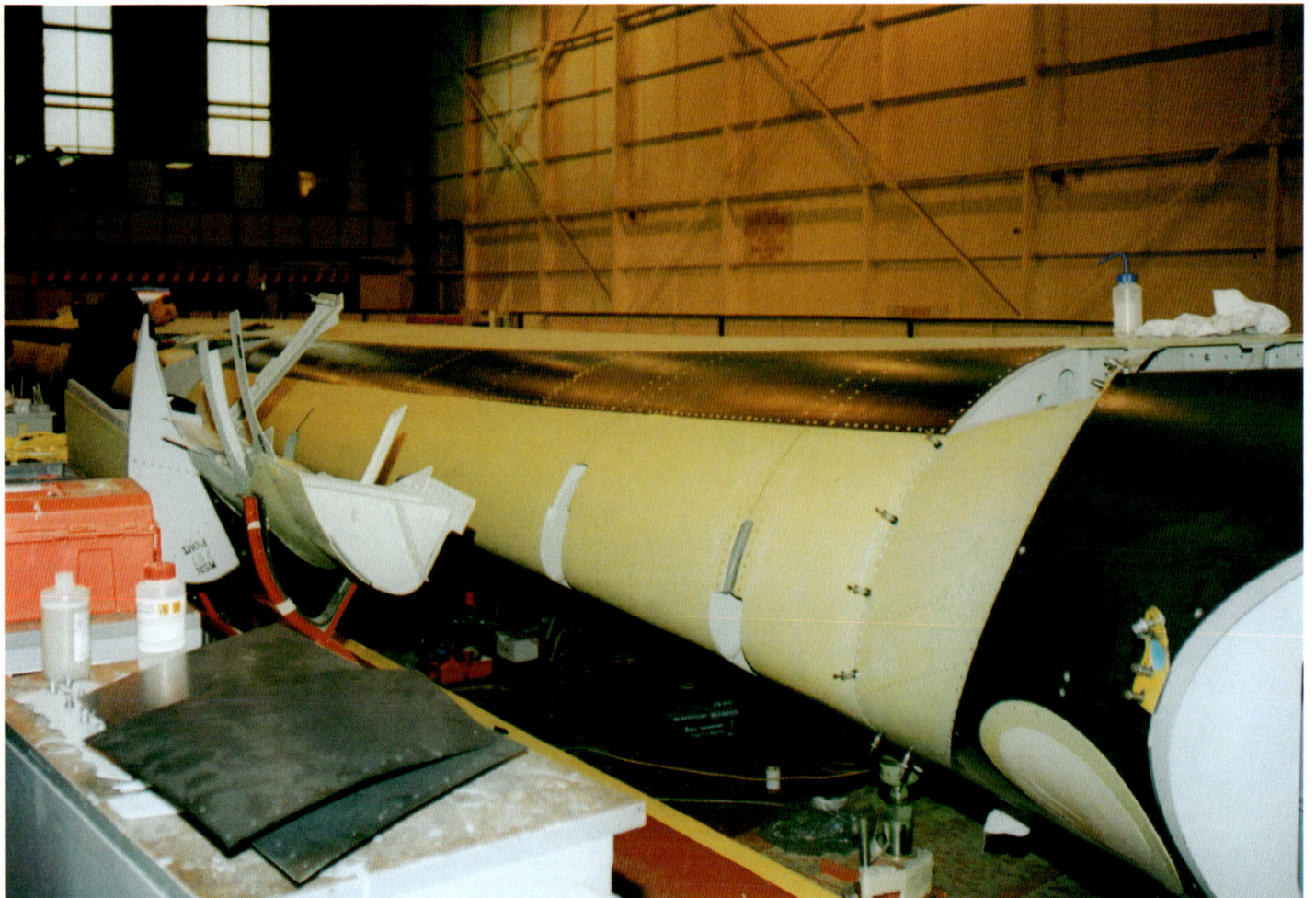

CONSTRUCTION

Something of the complexity of a modern passenger aircraft may be gauged from the description of its systems above. Constructing such a complex machine requires skill and precision, under pressure of time and constraints of budget. And while it may bear a single maker's name, an airliner is as likely as not the product of a collaborative effort by a large

Left: Conversion job. The airline business is never static; there are always modifications, upgrades and improvements to existing airframes that allow them to perform more efficiently in the role their owners need. Here, an Airbus A300 is converted to a freighter at Filton. Peter R. March

Below Left: Civil aircraft are no longer built in one location: many manufacturers, often all over the world, are involved in making components that are then assembled in one location. Here, Airbus wings are under construction at Chester: once finished, they will be flown to France for final assembly. Peter R. March

Below: This shows the BAe/Raytheon production line at Chester in the mid-1990s when the Hawker 800 and 1000 business jets were still built there. In the early 1990s, Raytheon bought BAe's Corporate Jet division and renamed the BAe125 -800 and -1000. Today, the -800 is built in Wichita (production of the -1000 ceased). Peter R. March

number of subcontractors, often in different countries, whose outputs must be carefully coordinated to ensure a smooth production process. Taking the Airbus fleet as an example, the wings are built in Britain, the fuselage in France, the tail surfaces in Germany and other parts in Belgium, while final assembly is at Toulouse in France. The Boeing 717 is produced from components and sub-assemblies made in nine different countries in North America, Europe, and Asia.

The "drawing board" has largely been eliminated from the design process. In fact, the Aerospatiale/BAC Concorde was the last aircraft to be designed solely by the human hand, and the process is now carried out almost exclusively on computers using CAD and 3D software. Computer hardware and software has made it possible to build a virtual aircraft, eliminating the need for large and expensive mock-ups and allowing the designers to evaluate components in a virtual environment. This is countered by the fact that airliners have increased in complexity by a very great degree,

ТУПОЛЕВ-334

The Aircraft

particularly the cabin interiors, and in certain areas of construction the task has become more difficult.

The number of individual components that must be integrated into the aircraft may run into millions, and the task of ordering, tracking, and distributing is an impressive feat of logistics. Construction materials range from the high-grade metal alloys used for the spars and skins, through composites, plastics, petroleum byproducts such as rubber and paint, to the fabric on the seats and floors, most of them specifically developed for the aerospace industry.

At the larger construction facilities such as Boeing's Everett and Renton plants, the aircraft are assembled from the major subassemblies in special bays equipped with jigs and support jacks, with walkways around the structure to ease access. The various subassemblies may be transported around the Everett building by overhead gantry cranes, and specially-built transporters bring fuselage sections from other Boeing facilities. Airbus has a special double-sized version of its A300, dubbed the Beluga, to transport completed wing sections across Europe.

A large airliner is built as a series of subassemblies, which are slotted together to form the aircraft. The fuselage is built in sections around ribs spaced at intervals along the length of the cabin, and onto which the sheet metal skin is riveted. The wing is similarly built around spars and ribs, onto which the skin is riveted after installation of certain components. The task of installing tens of thousands of metal rivets is time-consuming even with an automatic system such as that used by Boeing on the 777 wing. The major airframe subassemblies, including fuselage sections, wings, horizontal and vertical tail surfaces, engine pylons, flying surfaces, and undercarriage legs are mated prior to the installation of the complex electrical circuitry, plumbing, and powerplant systems. Installation of the electrical system is one of the most complex tasks, perhaps best demonstrated by the fact that an airliner may well contain over 150 miles of wiring. All in all, the construction process takes weeks. Finally, the aircraft arrives at the painting bay, where it gains its identity. It is then flight-tested to ensure that the systems are functioning properly prior to delivery.

Left: *The Tupolev Tu-334 started flight testing in 1998.* Peter R. March

Part 2

The People

The aircrew, comprising the flight and cabin crew, has the ultimate responsibility for the safe passage of the aircraft and its payload, and carries the burden of efficiently managing a hugely complex machine and its cargo. The process of choosing and training this highly professional body of individuals is exacting and rigorous—those who can satisfy the demands will be expected to maintain high standards of professionalism for so long as they stay in the role. Basic requirements are mental and physical aptitude and stability, along with interpersonal and management skills. Team players are actively sought—in the words of one big recruiter, "We don't want attitude or ego."

"Is it on autopilot?"

The captain is in overall command, but shares responsibility with the first officer—his second-in-command. On larger aircraft he may be assisted by the flight engineer, the purser (on certain long flights), the senior flight attendant, and by the

A number of major international airlines undertake training of their own pilot candidates either using existing training organizations, or, if they anticipate a long-term pilot requirement, they may form their own training college.

China Southern Airlines formed a joint venture in 1993 at Jandacot general aviation airfield near Perth in Western Australia called the China Southern West Australia Flying College (CSWAFC) to take advantage of the generally excellent weather conditions in the region for flight training, as well as developing the candidates' English language skills. It also meant that the students were able to qualify for an ICAO recognized commercial pilot's license (CPL).

The candidates are all students of the Beijing University of Aeronautics and Astronautics and the flight training is the practical part of the degree course. All trainees are employees of China Southern Airlines. The students arrive in Perth with no flying experience apart from as passengers on their flight to Australia, and the flight training is broken down into four phases, with an optional fifth phase for the more able students. A number of the photographs in this chapter look at this project.

Left: A total of 38 Grob G115C2 trainers are used in the first three phases with Phase 1 flown at Jandacot to solo standard including two hours consolidation. Phases 2 and 3 are flown at the less-congested company-owned airfield at Merredin some 150 miles east of Perth in the desert. Phase 2 consists of general handling competence such as stalling, steep turns, practice force landings, and some instrument flying. This leads to the completion of a General Flying Progress Test, which—if passed—moves the student on to Phase 3. This phase concentrates primarily on navigation skills, including radio communications and two hours of night-solo circuits culminating in achieving the CPL. This photograph shows a student during the PPL phase, learning to make the walk-around inspection of the aircraft to ensure it is fit for flight. Philip J. Birtles

junior flight attendants. It is sometimes wrongly assumed that modern technology has rendered the job of the pilot obsolete. Although it is certainly true that automated systems have reduced some of the workload and replaced the flight engineer, the skills of the pilot have not been diminished. In fact, in today's crowded skies, his alertness is perhaps doubly important, and effective management of the multitude of complex gadgetry equally so. Depending on the size of the operation, the pilot may also have other responsibilities such as loading and unloading the aircraft. Other non-flying duties routinely performed by pilots include record-keeping, flight scheduling, major maintenance scheduling, and minor repairs.

Flight crew

There are a number of paths available to the individual who wishes to pursue a career as a pilot in the field of civil aviation, and not all of them lead to a seat in the cockpit of a passenger airliner. Other areas of opportunity include flight instruction, air-freight, corporate aviation, and the air taxi business. The minimum requirement for pilots who are paid to transport passengers and cargo is a commercial transport pilot's license (CTP(L)) with instrument rating. However, the vast majority of registered pilots in the U.S. and Europe work for the airlines, for which an airline transport pilot's license is an additional requirement. The steps to each qualification—referred to by the FAA and the JAA as the CTP and CTP(L) and as the ATP and ATP(L)—are detailed below. Airlines still train and recruit flight engineers for their older aircraft, but two-man operation is becoming the norm as these are phased out.

Above Left: *A return is made to Jandacot for Phase 4, which starts with seven to ten hours' conversion to the twin-engine Cessna 310. The CSWAFC had a fleet of four Cessna 310s, which were replaced by five Piper Seneca Vs in April 2001. This student is making his first flight in the Cessna 310, learning to operate an aircraft with a retractable undercarriage, the synchronization of the engines, and stalling with the undercarriage raised and lowered.* Philip J. Birtles

Left: *Once a conversion has been made to the Cessna 310, the students complete about forty hours of training, covering navigation and instrument exercises, gaining a multi-engine commercial instrument rating with their CPL.* Philip J. Birtles

There are three main routes to a career in the cockpit of an airliner. The first is direct entry through one of the limited number of places available in airline training programs. The airline covers the cost of training from start to finish. It is usually of the highest quality, competition is predictably high, and the recruit may be expected to complete a mandatory period of employment with the operator after completing training.

The second approach is to fund the training oneself and gain the necessary qualifications at one of the countless flight training academies operating in the United States, United Kingdom, Australia, and South Africa (warm and dry locations, such as Florida and California, are favored because the prospect of interruptions due to poor weather are decreased). Taking this option may well cost $50,000, with no guarantee of employment at the end.

Third, airlines also recruit a significant number of ex-military pilots, particularly those with multi-engine experience. In the next ten years, there is likely to be a rising number of former military pilots entering the profession.

The cost of training flight crew to ATP(L) standard is high because of its length and complexity. No company would invest its hard-won capital in training an individual unless it could be confident in that person's ability to convert training into ability. Likewise, the less-than-fully-committed individual may balk at the prospect of investing a lot of borrowed money, with no guarantee of a job to pay back the loan. It comes as no great surprise that competition is high for places in the limited number of airline training programs, and with a glut of applicants to choose from, the airlines can afford to be selective. Only the largest of operators maintain their own training facilities. United Airlines has an impressive facility on the site of the former Stapleton Airport in Denver, and British Airways runs its own center at Cranebank, near London Heathrow Airport. Smaller operators usually sub-contract the work to larger airlines or else recruit trained personnel.

Selection

Any application is usually initiated by a formal letter, followed by an invitation to selection, or, for experienced pilots, an interview. Taking the British

Airways Sponsored Pilot Scheme as an example, applicants must meet certain basic academic and physical requirements, hold an unrestricted passport, and be under twenty-seven years of age at the time of application. Based on his formal letter of application, he may be asked to attend a two-day selection course, during which time he must demonstrate why he is deserving of a major financial commitment. The first day consists of classroom tests were his basic aptitude for flying, mental alertness, and dexterity are tested through written and computer based tests. Should these prove to be of an acceptable standard, on the second day the candidate is interviewed by a team including an experienced company line pilot and a member of the human resources department, and undergoes further testing. On successful completion of this interview, the applicant undergoes a thorough medical examination with the Civil Aviation Authority and BA's own medical staff before being offered a place in the training program. The course is designed to take the complete rookie through early training, although some applicants may have already gained some flight experience.

For the non-sponsored individual, it is a case of selecting a suitable flying school, and perhaps applying for a loan. Flight training is an industry in itself, and has spawned a great number of establishments that, for a fee, guarantee to take a candidate from rookie level through to the Multi Engine Commercial Instrument Flying Rating—the minimum requirement to transport passengers and cargo on a commercial basis, and a major step toward the ATP(L). The best centers offer pre-training aptitude assessments and individually tailored courses, and train with modern aircraft and computer simulation equipment. If it is assumed that the trainee already holds a PPL, the training typically takes 100-130 days on a full-time basis, for a cost of around $30,000.

Above Left: Originally the McDonnell Douglas MD11, the three-engined airliner entered service in the early 1990s but its career was cut short following takeover by Boeing. However, nearly 150 aircraft were built and they continue to fly, so pilot training is still essential—hence this new MD11 simulator at Fort Worth, Texas. Peter R. March

Left: Cockpit of a Brymon Dash 8-300, a twin-turboprop STOL airliner that can carry up to sixty passengers. Peter R. March

Flight training

Across the industry, training is increasingly reliant on simulators, which helps to reduce the pressure on flight scheduling and costs. However, at the basic level, training is still done in actual aircraft. Presuming he has no previous experience, the first stage of training is designed to take the pilot to a sufficient level of proficiency to hold a Private Pilot's License (PPL)—the first step on the route to the ATP(L). Although largely dependent on ability, this involves around thirty hours of ground and flying instruction, followed by ten hours of solo flying. Although it has its own training facility, BA sends its trainee pilots to selected flight training schools in England and the U.S. for training up to ATP(L) standard, and then takes over the reins for line training and type conversion. The ground school involves spending four to seven weeks in the classroom covering a range of topics from aerodynamics, meteorology, and engineering principles to navigation, radio operation, and aviation law. Flight training runs concurrently with the ground school and is divided in to three phases. The first covers single engine flight training designed to take the individual up to his first solo flight; the second phase involves an intensive period of integrated training in real aircraft and simulators and is followed by a third phase, which should leave the individual fully prepared for the Commercial Pilot's License Skill Test, and the examinations covering sixteen technical and navigation subjects. Finally, the student spends thirty hours flying a twin-engine aircraft, at the end of which he must face, usually with some trepidation, the Instrument Rating Test. Although initial training may take place in England, all trainees spend some time in the U.S., where more favorable weather conditions allow greater continuity in the training process.

This describes one of the more direct routes to the ATP(L). The non-sponsored pilots who make up the majority undergo similar PPL training at the school of their choice, perhaps having wisely consulted with a specialist recruiter and taken a medical examination to determine their suitability as a career pilot. PPL training costs around $3,500-$5,000, and this does not necessarily include accommodations, exam fees, and other expenses.

the number of specialist simulator training schools reflects this. Also, the support sectors of the larger aircraft manufacturing companies are now offering specially-tailored training programs to their customers.

Recruitment

Many airlines will only recruit experienced flight crew, or else those with flying experience such as former military pilots. This can be something of a barrier to newly trained pilots, who need work to gain experience—and vice-versa. Recruitment is undertaken through a number of channels, one of the most popular being the numerous specialist agencies with industry professionals on their books. These agencies will, to some extent, undertake the initial selection and interview processes themselves. The aviation industry print media, for example Flight International and the various trade publications, contain classified recruitment pages, as do the burgeoning number of online recruitment sites. Aircrew leasing is another expanding area of the industry, helping operators to fill short and long-term vacancies. Acceptance via BA's direct entry pilot program, which takes experienced crew up to the age of forty-nine, requires a full ATP(L) and MCC in addition to the standard JAA/CAA medical requirements. Applicants undergo a series of aptitude tests and those who are successful progress to a second stage, involving an interview with a Line Pilot and Human Resources consultant, followed by a simulator-based flying test. Depending on current operational demands, the individual may then be offered immediate employment, or else be offered a place in the "hold pool," a list of pilots that BA maintains and from which it can draw as needs arise. Another interesting scheme is offered by U.S.-based operator COMAIR, which guarantees any individual who successfully completes an ATP course with its subsidiary flight training center a job with the parent carrier.

Above: *Cabin crew are the public face of the airline and their training is rigorous and meticulous. Airline requirements from the crew can be very exacting.* Peter R. March

Below: *Seating for three non-flight deck crew on an Airbus A300 cargo. Specialized aircraft have developed to fill specialized roles and each requires a different layout and amenities.* Brian S. Strickland

Currently, airlines are experiencing a real shortage of experienced flight crew, which is likely to worsen over the next five years with many current ATP(L) holders slated for retirement. However, there will be considerable competition for jobs, as the number of applicants for new employment will exceed the number of openings.

Working Conditions

By law, airline pilots may not fly more than 100 hours in any one month or 1,000 hours per year. Most average around 75, and work an additional 75 hours a month on non-flying duties. Non-airline employees may have a much more irregular schedule, and fly 30 hours one month and 90 the next. For a long-haul pilot, long and irregular hours flying through many time zones wreaks havoc on the body clock and leads to continual tiredness—a common complaint among pilots and cabin crew. While flying does not require great physical effort, it is a mentally stressful task. Furthermore, the job often involves long periods spent away from home, which can be tough on family life. Divorce rates are fairly high in the industry. The various professional bodies that have been established to look after interests of airline employees have had some successes in improving pay and conditions, with occasional recourse to industrial action.

Career Development and Benefits

From the rank of First Officer, an airline pilot's career may progress through the ranks of Captain, Senior Training Captain, and perhaps even Chief Pilot. Alternatively, he may get out of commercial flying altogether and pursue a career is some aviation-related field, where his leadership and organizational skills will be a bonus. Some pilots leave to start their own training or charter organizations. The growing number of dignitaries and notaries who maintain their own personal aircraft may even seek his skills—the options are numerous.

Most pilots will readily admit to having flying in their blood and actively seek to maintain their involvement—both professional and personal—after retirement. Currently, the FAA and CAA require that ATP(L) holders retire at the age of sixty, when it is surmised (somewhat controversially) that an individual no longer has the necessary alertness of mind and an increased susceptibility to debilitat-

ing and incapacitating medical conditions. Unfortunately, this robs the profession of its most experienced flying personnel at a time when they are of great benefit to new trainees.

This brings us to the rewards and benefits enjoyed by the typical airline pilot, if indeed there is such as thing. Aside from the considerable prestige that is attached to the career, which in itself opens many doors, the pilot can expect to command a healthy salary from the start of his career to its conclusion. The typical starting salary for a First Officer with British Airways is about $40,000. This figure should rise progressively as the pilot builds hours and experience, and salary is generally commensurate with this. A captain flying long routes on a 747 or A340 will be commanding in excess of $75,000, and perhaps twice that figure. This obviously represents a "high point" and many pilots outside of Europe and the U.S. earn far less, but generally speaking, they are recognized to be highly-trained professionals with significant responsibilities and are rewarded accordingly. Aside from the financial rewards, the most obvious perk is the opportunity for travel. On long-haul networks the pilot may be able to enjoy long stopovers. Furthermore, the pilot and his immediate family enjoy concessionary travel with the airline and, through the Association of Travel Industry Employees, with other operators as well.

Future Prospects

As mentioned, the industry is experiencing something of a shortfall in pilots, which will be further exacerbated as passenger and freight traffic increases. The industry is looking hard at its recruitment strategies and actively seeking solutions. We are some way off from the pilotless airliner, although the technology is already in existence for such a machine. The presence of a highly-trained professional in the pilot's seat seems to provide a psychological reassurance that no machine can currently inspire.

Above Left: Flight attendant serves drinks on a BAC One-Eleven. Peter R. March

Left and Page 108: *Comparison between the 2 x 4 x 2 seating in economy class and the 2 x 2 x 2 of business class on an Aer Lingus A330.* Peter R. March

Cabin Crew

Although somewhat less demanding and expensive, training as a cabin crewmember is still a meticulous and exacting process. The basic demands for the hopeful, in what remains a female-dominated industry, are good interpersonal and organizational skills, physical fitness (conforming to FAA/CAA standards), and flexibility—some airlines require their cabin crew to live within thirty minutes of the operational hubs. Flight attendants are very much the public face of the airline for the greater part of the flight and it is by them that customers judge the airline.

The basic selection process involves application by letter to the airline human resources department. Eighteen is usually the minumum age required of an applicant. Applications are processed, and the candidates are called for an interview with management staff and experienced cabin crew. Some airlines emphasize foreign language skills, and experience in nursing or certain service industries may be an advantage. Recruitment staff will be looking to root out anyone who considers the career as a cheap and permanent holiday, although the opportunity for travel is recognized as a major incentive for applicants.

After completing the required medical (which precludes very short and very tall people, those with weight not in proportion to their height and those with mental or physical disabilities), trainees are schooled in a number of essential skills, including first aid, emergency procedures, customer service, and assertiveness training. First aid training is comprehensive, and generally supervised by a trained paramedic or company doctor. As well as the familiar cuts, burns, and CPR training, flight attendants should also be able to administer more complex medical aid. This training is designed to preserve life in the event of a serious accident or medical emergency in transit. Heart attacks are not uncommon on airliners, and more than one individual owes his life to the first aid skills of a flight attendant.

Probably the most rigorous part of training deals with emergency procedures. Because safety is so tightly regulated by the ICAO, which has the power to revoke an operator's license, these procedures are very thoroughly instilled in the crew, pilots included. They are trained to deal with minor

fires, in the operation of life jackets and rafts, and emergency beacons—all of the equipment that must by law be carried on a commercial passenger-carrying aircraft. One of the tests involves crawling through the smoke-filled mock-up of a cabin interior to the emergency exit, a disorienting and claustrophobic experience not recommended for the faint-hearted.

One of the personal qualities that cabin crew training seeks to develop is assertiveness, an obvious asset in a challenging situation and one that will be recognized by anyone who has traveled with a group of troublemakers or an intoxicated individual. Cabin crew are regularly required to deal with troublesome and awkward passengers and must have the confidence, authority, and diplomacy to resolve such confrontations as may arise. Again, assertiveness will be a natural asset in an emergency, where discipline can easily break down.

The final aspect of training deals with the actual mechanics of the job—operating the galley equipment, doors, and entertainment systems, drink and meal preparation, and service. After formal testing of this knowledge, the trainee is usually assigned to a particular aircraft type or family, and is expected to know the location of each and every piece of equipment on it. Refresher training is undertaken annually.

Responsibilities

Primarily, the flight attendant is responsible for the safety and care of the passengers. This includes ensuring that they are properly positioned during takeoff, landing, and if turbulent conditions are encountered, briefed as to the location of personal emergency equipment and emergency doors and their correct operation, and the correct stowage of baggage in the passenger cabin. Flight attendants may sometimes also have to protect passengers from themselves and others. Excessive alcohol consumption is a threat to the safety of the aircraft, and violent arguments between friends, family, and strangers are by no

means uncommon. This phenomenon, popularly known as "Air Rage," is yet another challenge for today's cabin crew.

The boarding and disembarkation of the passengers often has to be accomplished in a relatively short time period, particularly on short routes where rapid turnarounds help to maximize operational efficiency. During turnaround the aircraft must be cleaned, its galleys restocked, and a mandatory security check undertaken. All of these responsibilities fall to the cabin crew. The cleaning task is performed either by a specialized team at the airport or by the cabin crew themselves. In the former case, the cabin is checked by the crewmembers before it is approved by the senior attendant. To some extent the task has been eased by the smoking ban imposed by most major airlines, but it is not the most popular of tasks all the same. During turnaround or else before they are released, the crew also performs a security sweep of the aircraft to check for any forgotten items of luggage or clothing and, more importantly, for suspicious packages.

During the flight itself, the crew performs additional duties such as serving refreshments, operating the on-board entertainment systems, distributing reading materials and headphones, and operating the onboard shop. Their first concern remains passenger safety and here they must use good judgement when distributing drinks.

Rewards and Benefits

Salaries vary greatly in this branch of the industry. A new recruit to an U.K.-based charter operation can expect a basic salary in the region of $12,000, with additional flight pay adding another $7,500. Good performance in the job may lead to a promotion to senior flight attendant status, with a corresponding salary raise, and then on to chief flight attendant and even purser. The purser on a long-range wide-body jet is in charge of up to thirty-five people, and the name is taken, like so many in the aviation world, from the maritime dictionary of terms. Cabin crew usually benefit from the same concessionary travel as flight crew, and suffer from the same disruption to their sleep patterns, but there are none of the equivalent recruitment problems here and competition for the better jobs can be strong.

Above Left, Left, and Page 106: Comparison between the 2 x 4 x 2 seating in economy class and the 2 x 2 x 2 (Above left) of business class on an Aer Lingus A330. Peter R. March

Part 3

Maintenance

Regular maintenance, of which inspection and appropriate repair are functions, is a mandatory requirement of aircraft ownership and operation at all levels, and only when it is undertaken to the satisfaction of approved inspectors will an aircraft be considered airworthy and licensed for operation. The who, where, what, and how of commercial transport aircraft maintenance, preventive maintenance, rebuilding, and alteration is strictly governed in the U.S. by Parts 43 and 125 of the FAR, and in Europe by the JAA.

A certificate of airworthiness is subject to regular review and is also dependent on compliance with such directives as may be issued by the governing authority concerning that aircraft type, which require modification to some part of the aircraft or its service schedule. Alternatively, modification may be required as part of a fleet upgrade program, or else to adapt the aircraft to a new role. The tasks of inspection, repair, and modification fall within the remit of the huge maintenance and engineering services that support the aviation industry. The maintenance business is worth a great deal of money—more than is generated annually by the sales of aircraft, and is one of the major industry employment sectors.

Personnel

Aircraft maintenance and inspection personnel have usually gained some basic technical knowledge or qualification in mechanical or electronic engineering at school, or at least a grounding in science-based subjects, before embarking on a career in aviation engineering/maintenance.

For FAA certification as an airframe mechanic (who may work on any part of the aircraft except the powerplant, propellers, and avionics), powerplant mechanic (limited to working on engines and some propeller work), or avionics repair specialist, a basic requirement for someone training "on the job" straight from school is at least

Left: *KLM engine maintenance.* Peter R. March

eighteen months of hands-on experience, or thirty months for a combined Airframe and Powerplant qualification (which covers all parts of the aircraft except the instruments). The individual licenses are awarded dependent on the successful completion of appropriate oral and written tests. It is possible, however, to circumvent this requirement by completing a program at a FAA-certified mechanic school. In the U.S., the vast majority of mechanics train at one of over 200 trade schools, which award two to four year degrees in avionics, aviation technology, or aviation service management. Students must complete a minimum of 1,900 hours of formal training, during which time they will be taught the principles of aviation technologies, now with increasing emphasis on turbine engines, composite materials, and avionics.

A & P holders make up the vast majority of the 130,000 registered aircraft mechanics in the U.S., and this certification and a high school diploma is usually a mandatory requirement for an airline. They may work on one or many different types of aircraft, although they must also hold authorization for the type of aircraft or engine on which they are currently working. There are also specialists in different fields such as hydraulics and electrics.

After a minimum of three years gaining experience as an A & P mechanic, an individual may apply for an inspector's certificate, which allows him to certify maintenance and repair work performed by others, and to complete scheduled inspections. Promotion then follows a path to lead inspector and shop supervisor, and perhaps to an executive position with an airline or a role as a government (FAA) inspector.

All holders of any FAA mechanic qualification must complete at least 1,000 hours of work experience each year to keep his license valid and undergo sixteen hours of refresher training every two years.

The best-paid mechanics are usually those working on jets for the airlines, where they may command $25 an hour for their services. All the work is often quite physical, and may be carried out in cramped, smelly, dirty, and noisy conditions.

Left: *The nose radar of a KLM Boeing 747 receiving attention.*
Peter R. March

Right: *KLM engine maintenance.*
Peter R. March

Mechanics often work under pressure of time, yet have a great responsibility for safety, and this can cause the job to be stressful. In the U.S., about two-thirds of all mechanics work for the airlines, and most of the rest work for the manufacturers, with a small proportion employed by the FAA and independent repair stations.

Facilities

Most airlines have their own maintenance facilities or repair stations, which are usually located at the airline's base or at a convenient airport. They may alternatively subcontract all or part of the work to a licensed repair station. The larger organizations are equipped to offer a wide range of services such as airframe overhaul; others specialize in specific aircraft system, such as hydraulics, avionics, powerplant, or fuel. Also offered are detailed planning and review of airline maintenance schedules, and coordination of maintenance activities.

The work that a certified repair station may perform is regulated by Part 145 of the FAR, and they perform maintenance according to the owner's manual or schedule for ongoing airworthiness compiled by the manufacturer for the aircraft type (which is, in turn, approved by the regulatory authority). They must also administer the maintenance record. The details of any work that is carried out must be entered into this record, along with the signature of the person who has approved the work.

All maintenance, repair, and inspection work is completed according to a prescribed order, to prevent any confusion and to allow one worker to hand over a task to another. In what is potentially a dangerous working environment, aircraft mechanics must be safety-conscious.

Inspection and Maintenance

Inspection and maintenance is a never-ending process over the entire lifespan of the aircraft and a responsibility of many people, including the crew. Before they take charge of the aircraft, the crew is informed of any problems, and one of the flight crew makes a visual inspection of the aircraft exterior. During the flight itself, they monitor the systems for any sign of malfunction, which will be reported upon arrival and action taken to rectify the problem. This process of monitoring, which has been improved in recent years by the installation of onboard electronic monitoring systems, is supplemented at regular intervals during the aircraft's life by preventive maintenance and routine inspections at an approved facility, and by "heavy" maintenance at longer intervals and by repair and modification work as necessary. All aircraft are required to undergo statutory inspection, but ultimately it is the responsibility of the operator to ensure that they are safe to operate. Finally, before it can be returned to service, the aircraft must be inspected and tested and the work approved by a certified inspector.

Large transport aircraft are maintained according to an ongoing schedule based on the requirements of the manufacturer's maintenance schedule, the operator's own schedule, and the requirements of the regulating authority. Mostly this consists of preventive maintenance, as opposed to repair, which involves the systematic inspection and replacement of parts. This may typically include examination of engines, landing gear, instruments, pressurized sections, accessories, brakes, pumps, valves, and air-conditioning systems. A well-equipped repair station will have equipment to test all of these components, or else subcontract the work to a specialist or the component manufacturer. Although the maintenance may in certain circumstances be performed outside, most facilities are equipped with bays that allow for easy access over the aircraft structure, and engines have specially designed inspection hatches.

Routine inspections consist of visual examination of the aircraft before each flight, its components and its systems, without the need for disassembly. At regular intervals, depending on a schedule based on the number of flying hours, calendar days, or cycles of operation, a more detailed inspection involving a more thorough examination is required, and most likely will require the disassembly of the relevant component or system. This may involve removing the powerplant, and using x-ray and magnetic inspection equipment to check for cracks in the turbine blades, and checking for the correct operation of hydraulic

Left: Delta maintenance hangar at Atlanta showing a Lockheed L1011 Tristar undergoing maintenance. Both: Peter R. March

and pneumatic systems components such as brake actuators, anti-skid devices, and pressure valves.

The checks vary in scope and are categorized A, B, C, and D Check Inspections, with a D check being the most involved. During these inspections, parts are tested to ensure that their operation and tolerances are within manufacturer's guidelines. However, certain components have a specified life, after which they must be replaced regardless of condition. At longer intervals, deep maintenance is undertaken, which requires for structures that are normally inaccessible to be examined, overhauled, repaired, or replaced as necessary. The engines are treated as separate to the airframe and have their own maintenance scheduling, again based on the number of operating hours.

Corrosion Prevention and Control

As part of the process of preventive maintenance, an airliner will also be inspected regularly for corrosion as part of a Corrosion Prevention and Control Program. Because of the environment in which they operate, the high-grade alloys that are used to build the basic airframe are susceptible to corrosion, particularly in humid conditions and after exposure to saltwater. A very graphic demonstration of this problem involved a 737 of Aloha Airlines, which lost a large section of its cabin roof and one of the crew members during a short island hop in the Hawaiian chain because of the combined effects of poorly monitored corrosion, airframe age, and abnormally high cabin pressurization cycles. Properly implemented, a corrosion prevention and control program will prevent the occurrence of corrosion, or else detect it at an early stage and ensure that remedial measures are taken.

Structural and Stress Analysis

Monitoring structural integrity is an important and highly sophisticated function of preventive maintenance as abnormal loads, metal fatigue, or corrosion may compromise the structural integrity of the aircraft.

Left: *Delta maintenance hangar at Atlanta showing a Boeing 757 (Above Left) and a Boeing 737—emphasizing the skills needed to keep such a varied fleet in the skies.* Peter R. March

The actual limits of the aircraft structure are found by subjecting it to stresses that are far in excess of those it will encounter under normal flight conditions, until it breaks. Operating restrictions such as G-forces and speed are imposed for each aircraft, which must not be exceeded in normal operations. Although every aircraft structure has a built-in margin of safety beyond its certified limits, should the aircraft exceed those G limits in operation, it will be examined in detail before it is allowed to fly again.

Metal fatigue was first researched extensively in the 1950s, in the wake of a series of fatal crashes involving the Comet jetliner. It is now understood more thoroughly that metal which is subjected to stress may weaken over time. As the life span of the aircraft may be quite considerable, it is necessary at intervals—particularly with older or high time aircraft—to check the structure for signs of metal fatigue.

The most highly stressed part of a turbine-powered aircraft is the engine turbine itself, which routinely endures enormous loads. Because of this, the turbine—and most particularly the blades—are regularly examined for signs of cracking or stretching, a phenomenon known as "creep" that occurs over time because of the combined effects of heat and centrifugal force.

Tools

The equipment that is used to maintain aircraft would take up a book in itself, and ranges from the most humble $5 screwdriver to a $30,000 test bench. There are specialized tools and test apparatus for hundreds of different jobs, some of which require special training. A mechanic must also keep a careful account of the tools that he is using, to prevent any from getting accidentally lost in the structure (it does happen!), make sure they are in good condition, and use them properly. Because of the inaccessibility of various parts the aircraft structure, the engineering industry has adopted a piece of equipment originally developed for surgery. The borescope allows the operator to examine hidden structures without first having to remove the overlying structures, and comprises a miniature lens at the end of a thin probe, which is linked to a camera by fiber optic cable. The probe is fed in through an access hole, and the image projected onto a TV

Maintenance

screen. This tool is particularly useful for examining engine internals.

As in other sectors of the industry, computer technology has had a major impact. Convenient CD-ROMs are replacing the bulky paper maintenance manuals that mechanics work from, and online services allow mechanics to access manufacturers records with greater ease.

Finally, for experimental and test work on components, manufacturers in the U.S. are able to call upon the extensive NASA facilities, which includes equipment to simulate "icing" and high speed wing tunnels to analyze aerodynamic performance and also a large archive of research data. Both the FAA and CAA also operate their own research facilities.

Repair

Depending on the results of a maintenance check or inspection, repairs may be needed to the avionics or mechanical components of the aircraft, or else to the structure itself. Mechanics specializing in repair work usually rely on the pilots, or the monitoring system, for a description of the problem.

Mechanical Components

This covers a very wide spectrum from the windscreen wiper assemblies to the galley and toilet plumbing, and comprises the greater part of the internal workings of the aircraft. As previously mentioned, many repair facilities specialize in one or more of these fields, such as hydraulics. Problems may occur in something as small as a pressure valve or a larger item such as a main gear strut, and the scope of the repair varies greatly. Components are removed from the airframe or engine, disassembled, cleaned, repaired (or replaced), and tested before being approved for return to service. The manufacturer generally carries out engine repairs or else it is dealt with by licensed subsidiaries. As part of this process it is normal for the complete engine to be removed.

Above Left and Left: Delta maintenance hangar at Atlanta showing work on Boeing 737s and Tristars (Above Left) and a Boeing 767 (Left). Peter R. March

Avionics Components

Repair and maintenance of avionics systems, navigation and communications equipment, weather radar, and other electronic flight instrumentation systems and computers that control flight, powerplant, and primary functions, takes up an increasingly large proportion of the maintenance process, and requires the specialized knowledge of a licensed avionics technician. Because of the complexity of these systems, additional training and licensing is often required, in addition to the standard avionics qualifications such as a FCC radiotelephone license.

Structural

Major structural repairs require specialized equipment and tooling for the fabrication and restoration of high-grade metal alloys and composite materials. Composites (carbon fiber, kevlar, boron, and glass fiber) are being used with more frequency in aircraft construction, and repairing them requires special bonding techniques as well as air-conditioned cleanrooms, vacuum cabinets, and ovens. Sheet, cast, and forged metal repair and fabrication requires welding, brazing, and manipulation tools, as well as larger equipment such as furnaces, quenching tanks, and a deep freeze for certain metal treatments, along with a host of precision measuring and test equipment.

Modifications

Periodically, the governing authority or national government may issue an order, known as an Airworthiness Directive, requiring the owners of a certain aircraft type to make a modification. This may be prompted by the findings of accident investigators, the age of the aircraft, or new noise regulations. Such an instance would perhaps involve heavy structural modifications (new wing spars, etc.) to a thirty-year-old aircraft. This is particularly relevant to operators of older aircraft in the U.S., which must now comply with stringent noise regulations requiring the fitting of hush kits or a complete engine overhaul to comply with the tougher European regulations.

Alternatively, the aircraft may require modification from passenger to freight configuration, involving the installation of larger cargo doors, cabin tie downs, and blanking the passenger windows. This work is routinely carried out on

Maintenance

older aircraft—such as 727s, DC–10s, and Tristars—disposed of by passenger carriers that are reequipping with more modern types.

On the flight deck, new avionics may require integration (see "Ground Proximity Warning System") as they become available. Reconfiguration of the passenger cabin is also carried out to meet differing requirements such as upgrade to VIP or Corporate standards, or just routine refurbishment.

Coatings

After a period of exposure to the ravages of the environment, even tough aircraft paint begins to lose its luster, and more importantly, its ability to protect against corrosion. Repainting may also be required when the aircraft changes hands on the secondhand market, or when the operator changes their color scheme. To add to this, airliners are now being used as flying billboards by the advertising industry, and by their owners. Painting shops are housed in large, environmentally controlled buildings, with dust filters and heaters to bake the paint after application. Bare metal sprays are obviously more involved than oversprays, but both require careful surface preparation to ensure proper bonding of the paint, which is applied in multiple layers of differing composition.

Spares

The two industry giants both have well-developed global spares and technical support services. In such a competitive market, airlines seek to reduce the time that an aircraft is out of service to the bare minimum, so the speedy and efficient dispatching of spares coupled with on-site technical assistance is essential.

As Boeing and Airbus have identified, the level of support that is on offer has an influence on orders,

Left: *At least with the small ones, you don't have to climb ladders! Engine maintenance is, of course, essential for aircraft of all sizes; shown here is a Piper Aztec.* Peter R. March

and both offer a package of ongoing support to prospective owners. Boeing has distribution centers for spares strategically located in Amsterdam, Atlanta, Bejing, Dubai, London, Los Angeles, Seattle, and Singapore, and employs a large staff of support personnel. These support activities cover not only spare parts, but also technical assistance, upgrades to older aircraft, heavy maintenance, and engine repair.

Airlines are now looking at the cost of aircraft purchase and operation over the whole lifespan, and provision of this type of after-sales support will become an increasingly significant factor. The support sector, of which maintenance is a major part, is set to enjoy healthy growth as the world aircraft fleet increases in size over the next twenty years.

Left: *"Deep" maintenance for a Northwest Boeing 747 at Minneapolis-St. Paul, the airline's home. One of the largest airlines in the world, Northwest runs a wide range of aircraft from 747s to Airbuses.* Peter R. March

Below Left and Below: *Northwest 747 gets a respray at Minneapolis-St. Paul.* Peter R. March

Managing the world's airspace is an extremely complex business, involving significant levels of international cooperation and investment.

As the volume of air traffic continues to increase year by year, the need to minimize delays and increase safety becomes more urgent and many new initiatives are being proposed and tested. The development of satellite technology and the continuous improvement of telecommunications and digital message handling is already being realized in improved efficiency.

The main organization responsible for the management of air traffic and its control is the International Civil Aviation Organization, ICAO, based in Montreal, Canada, which was established in 1946 by representatives of several nations. Another important contributor to airspace management is the International Air Transport Association, IATA. Most of the initiatives which are being developed to improve the world's aviation transport system are proposed by these organizations, who also take a leading role in undertaking safety audits for each country.

In Europe, a separate organization for the safety of air navigation was established in 1960, representing most European nations. This body, EUROCONTROL, based in Brussels, is now a driving force in the integration and cooperation between more than forty countries in the region. Europe is a particularly complex area of the world as far as air traffic is concerned, since many different systems have to be operated in a compact area where a significant proportion of the traffic is either climbing or descending, which produces a very busy control situation.

Left: *The Terminal Control Room at LATCC.*
Airsys ATM

Airspace

The airspace around the world consists of two basic types, controlled and uncontrolled. Controlled airspace is often referred to by the more general term "regulated airspace," since certain rules and regulations apply. The classification of airspace has been established with seven categories from Class A to Class G, with the Class A being subject to the highest degree of control and regulation and Class G being subject to very basic rules with virtually no control involvement.

Left: *The London and Area Terminal Control Center at West Drayton.* National Air Traffic Services Limited (NATS)

Below Left: *An aerial view of the new center at Swanwick, Hampshire.* NATS

Below: *An extract from the Jeppesen VFR chart used for low level flights.* Jeppesen

Most passenger flights operate in controlled airspace where the air traffic controller has legal responsibility for ensuring that aircraft remain separated by the minimum prescribed standards.

Where aircraft operate in remote areas of the world, or in oceanic regions, the control of traffic is handled in a way that is very different from that which applies over populated areas. This is primarily due to the fact that radar surveillance is limited and aircraft cannot be monitored accurately when they are beyond radar range. The highest degree of control is Class A airspace which essentially is applied to lower airspace around airports and groups of airports (referred to as Terminal Areas) and to ten-mile-wide routes which are defined by radio navigation beacons for commercial air traffic, known as Airways. Air space is also classified as "lower" and "upper," although different countries apply the split at varying levels. In the U.K., the separation between lower and upper airspace is at Flight Level 245, which is equal to 24,500 feet. The airways system that operates

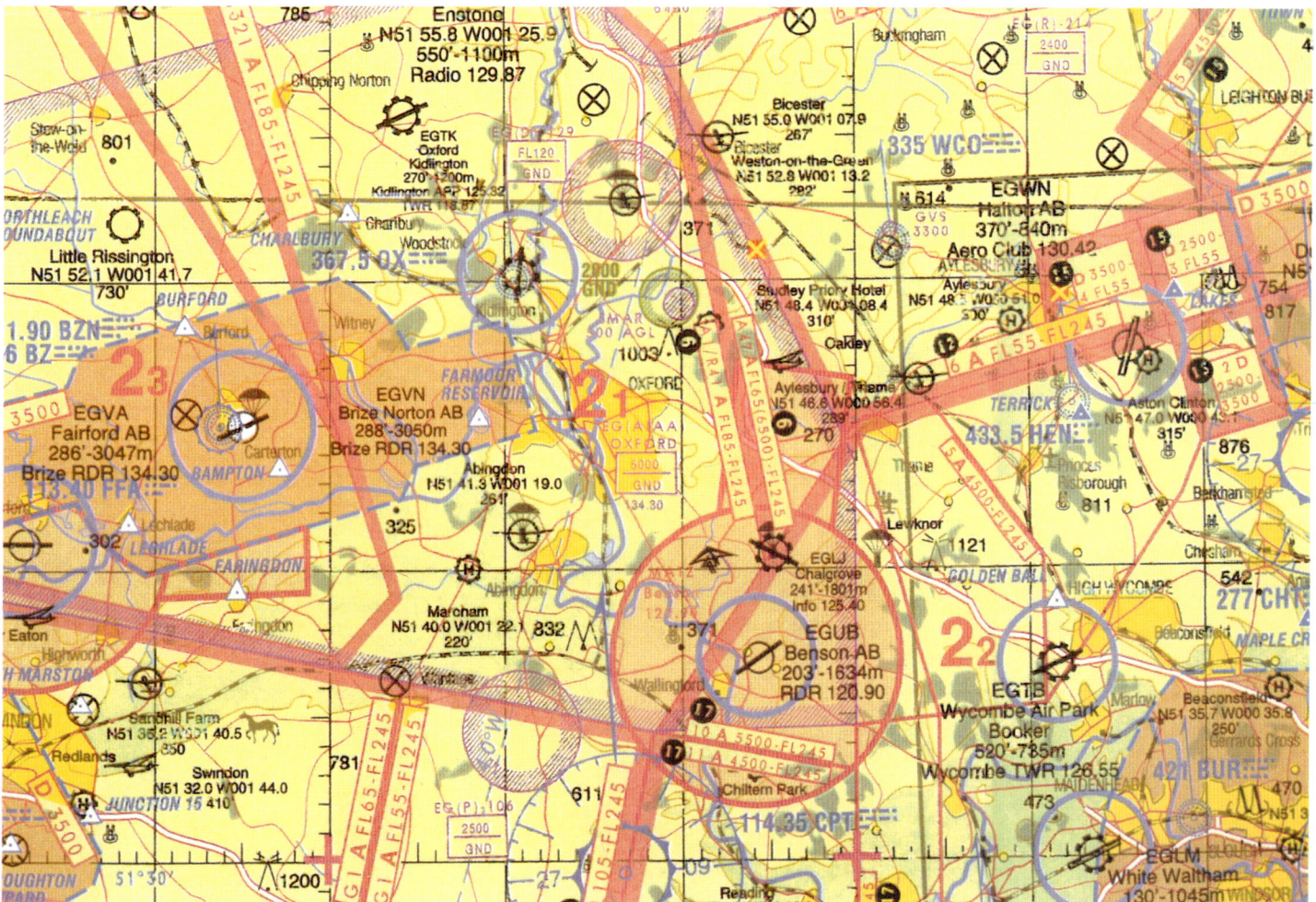

throughout Europe and in most other countries exists in lower airspace. In upper airspace a similar route structure is in place, except that the controlled airspace does not have any lateral limitations. In other words, all airspace above FL245 is under the control of the air traffic management organizations.

Control

The control process consists of spoken messages transmitted between air traffic control units and pilots using Very High Frequency radio in the range between 118 megahertz and 137 megahertz. As the flight crosses from one region to the next, the radio frequency is changed so that the pilot then speaks to the next controller.

Military pilots are also controlled in a similar manner, except that the radio frequency range is in the Ultra High Frequency band between 225 and 400 megahertz.

However, in remote areas or in oceanic airspace, since VHF radio operates on a line of sight basis, it cannot be used; therefore high frequency radio (also known as shortwave) is used. Modern developments in this field are now having an effect on oceanic traffic where the reporting of positions is increasingly being made through digital technology using satellites.

The messages which are passed between ground control and pilots have to be very carefully constructed so as to avoid any possibility of misunderstanding and confusion. International standard phrases are extensively used, but even with very careful planning there are still a significant number of risk-bearing incidents which occur every year,

Left: *The Visual Control Room and Airport Radar at Heathrow.* Graham Duke

Below Left: *A view of a new radar display to be used at Swanwick.* NATS

Below: *Approach controllers at Teesside.* NATS

often due to careless radio usage on the part of the pilot or the controller.

The normal method of control within Class A airspace is with the support of radar, enabling the controller to have a clear picture of all the traffic within the area of responsibility. Modern technology permits the controller to modify the information on the screen so as to present only the information which is relevant. For example, he can omit aircraft on the display for which he is not responsible by the use of filters which eliminate unnecessary signals. All aircraft which operate in controlled airspace have a facility for transmitting a four character number in response to a signal sent out by the radar scanner. This number, which is

referred to as the "squawk," is linked to the aircraft's flight plan and this enables the display to show the actual flight number on the radar screen. In addition, more information is available concerning the level of the aircraft and an indication as to whether it is climbing or descending. Modern equipment enables the transponders on different aircraft to communicate with each other electronically and for this information on surrounding traffic to be displayed to the pilots, together with any warnings about possible conflicts which may be several minutes ahead.

In areas of regulated airspace, where the rules are not as stringent as in Class A, the controller's role may be limited to the provision of advisory messages to the pilot, or, to a lesser extent, simply relaying information about other traffic. In these circumstances the responsibility for remaining clear of other traffic does not rest with the controller, but with the pilot.

Where the benefit of radar does not exist, or where the radar facility has failed, the control of

Left: *The Visual Control Room at Zurich.* Airsys ATM

Below Left: *The Terminal Control Room at LATCC.* Airsys ATM

Below: *Aberdeen Approach Controllers.* NATS

traffic is undertaken through a system known as "procedural control," where the pilot provides position reports and estimated times for future positions to the controller, who then ensures that other flights do not conflict. Procedural control also operates in remote regions or oceanic airspace which are beyond the range of radar; again position reports from pilots provide the basic information to ensure that flights remain safely apart. Where high frequency radio is employed, it is usual for radio operators to speak to the pilots and then relay the messages through to a control center where decisions on any changes in level or speed are taken.

Navigation Beacons

The original system of providing pilots with information about their positions was based on a network of radio navigation beacons transmitting a coded message in morse which identified the location, together with the magnetic bearing, of the aircraft from that point. Many thousands of radio beacons exist around the world and they are still used extensively by pilots to ensure that they remain confident about their position, although modern flight management computers, which receive position information from satellites, are rapidly becoming the main method of accurate long-range navigation. Although the basic structure of the airways is still dependent on radio navigation facilities, many flights today operate independently through their onboard management equipment.

Navigation beacons are given names that often relate to their locality. For example, in the U.K., some of the beacons that have been in position for many years bear the name of the local town or community. Examples are "Dover," "Clacton," "Lands End," "Ottringham," "Wallasey," and "Brecon." Each of these has a unique radio frequency and a coded three-letter identifier which indicates the precise location when the aircraft receiver is tuned to that particular beacon. "Dover," for example, sends out a continuous morse signal of the letters DVR on frequency 114.95.

Above Left: *Manchester Control Center.* Airsys ATM

Left: *The Terminal Control Room at LATCC.* Airsys ATM

Right: *VHF radio transmitter.* Graham Duke

Modern flight management equipment, however, can be programmed with the latitude and longitude coordinates of the individual navigation beacons and the computer will automatically direct the aircraft along the route from one position to the next. As the use of radio beacons declines for international air transport, many other locations have been established in upper airspace without the benefit of any equipment on the ground. These are now identified as "significant points" and all of these have five letters. Due to the very large number that are now used, they can no longer be given place names and most are simply a collection of letters which form the word. Examples of these are GINIS, INLAK, NIGIT, RATUK, and VABIK. These positions are now used by most international flights, and again the flight management computer will be programmed with their coordinates enabling the aircraft to follow a route entirely independent of the radio-based navigation beacons.

Levels

The way in which an aircraft maintains a particular vertical level is through the use of the altimeter, a device on board the aircraft which is sensitive to air pressure. A column of air exerts a particular pressure on the surface of the earth, but as the altitude increases the pressure becomes less and less and this difference can be measured. However, the complication that arises is the ever-changing air pressure around the earth from high to low and back again and this means that the altimeter is continually measuring changing circumstances. To overcome this, the altimeter has to be set to the local air pressure for any specific location and this reading is passed on to the pilot by the ground controller.

The air pressure is measured at mean sea level and this information is then passed on to the pilot using a term which was originally developed when morse code was in use, known as QNH. When the pilot sets the altimeter to the local QNH pressure, the instrument reads in feet above mean sea level. If,

Left: *A typical U.K. radar and radio installation for Air Traffic.* NATS

Right: *Clee Hill long range station.* Graham Duke

Right: *Radio Transmitters, Heathrow.* Graham Duke

Below: *Great Dunn Fell long-range radar.* Graham Duke

for example, a particular airfield is at 600 feet above sea level, the altimeter will read 600 when the aircraft is on the runway.

However, when the pressure is converted to the airfield level, the altimeter will read zero when the aircraft is on the runway. In this case the local air pressure is referred to as the QFE and this takes into account the difference in pressure between mean sea level and the distance of the runway above sea level. As air pressure decreases by one millibar for approximately every 30 feet above sea level, this will provide a QFE reading which will be 20 millibars lower than the QNH reading where, of course, the runway is at 600 feet AMSL. The difference between the two readings will always be the same for the same airport. The only situation where the QNH pressure and the QFE pressure are the same will be when the runway is at sea level.

For high-level, long-range flights, the changing air pressure would mean that to maintain an accurate level, the pilot would need to continuously change the setting on the altimeter in order to maintain accuracy. This, of course, would be extremely difficult to achieve and would be a risky operation as so many other flights would be in the area. This problem is overcome by an internationally agreed barometric pressure setting of 1013.2 millibars which is used by all aircraft operating at high level regardless of the actual air pressure in the area. When an aircraft is flying with a pressure setting of 1013.2, the level is described as a Flight Level and the last two digits of the level are omitted. For example, 35,000 feet would be described as FL350, 12,000 feet would be described as FL120 and 8,000 feet would be described as FL80.

However, where the pressure setting is based on actual pressure using the QNH and QFE readings, these are described as "altitude" and "height," respectively. Altitude indicates the level of the aircraft above mean sea level, whereas height indicates the level of the aircraft above the runway of the particular airport in question.

In many parts of the world, the pressure measurement system is in inches of mercury, 29.92 inches being equivalent to 1013.2 millibars.

Airports
Airports and airfields vary tremendously in their complexity and in the volume of traffic which they handle. A small local airfield will obviously operate to a much lower level of control and activity when compared to a large international airport dealing with many hundreds of aircraft movements every day, often involving several runways at the same time.

Runways are identified by reference to the magnetic bearing in degrees, rounded up or down to the nearest ten degrees with the final zero omitted. At Heathrow, for example, where the runways face east and west, they have the identifiers 27 and 09. As there are two parallel runways, these are also identified as left and right.

Small airfields do not have any sophisticated facilities for dealing with flights and many will be dealt with by the employment of flight information service officers or radio operators instead of air traffic controllers.

However, at a large airport the volume of traffic makes it necessary to subdivide the different areas of control and handling so that the radio frequencies do not become congested. The number of aircraft that a controller can handle at any one time is largely dependent on the time taken to transmit voice messages to the pilot and for the pilot to read back the confirmation of the correct details. Methods to shorten these processes are used to enable more aircraft to be dealt with within the same space of time.

At a large airport the ATC functions will be separated as shown below.

Delivery
This controller will give the pilot permission to start engines and will also give basic information regarding the cleared route. Departures from large airports are arranged by specifying the precise turning points and different levels to be achieved at each position to take the aircraft away from the airfield and on to the initial route for its journey. These are known as Standard Instrument Departures, abbreviated to SIDs, and are identified by navigation beacons which may be many miles away from the airport. The SID is also given a number and a letter which the pilot uses to confirm that the flight management computer has been correctly loaded with the exact details. As an example, a Standard Instrument Departure from Heathrow to the southeast would be to the navigation beacon at Dover.

The controller, when issuing the first message to the pilot would refer to this route and to the aircraft callsign. For example, "Speedbird 11, start up approved for Singapore, Dover 3 Juliet, squawk 5225." This very short message provides the pilot with everything he needs to start his journey. He has clearance to start engines and his route will be specified for him on one of his charts as being via Dover. The word "Juliet" indicates the departure runway in use at Heathrow as 09 right. The pilot will then change radio frequency to receive his next instructions.

Left and Below Left: *Inside and outside views of the venerable air traffic control tower at London Heathrow, festooned with aerials and dishes.* Peter R. March

Below: *Manchester Visual Control Room.* NATS

Ground

This controller will give the pilot permission to have the aircraft pushed back from its stand ready to taxi out to the departure runway which in our example is 09 right. Once the engines are running and the aircraft is ready to start, the ground controller will be contacted and his clearance will then be passed to the pilot. For example, "Speedbird 11 push is approved face to the west." Once the aircraft has been pushed back from its stand, the pilot will request taxi instructions and these will also be given by the ground controller. For example, "Speedbird 11 cleared to taxi follow the inner taxiway for 09 right." Once the aircraft has taxied across the airport and is approaching the line of other aircraft waiting for departure, the ground controller will give the instruction to change frequency to the departure controller. Red stoplights will prevent the aircraft from taxiing too far.

Departures

The departure controller, as the name suggests, deals only with departing flights. As soon as the aircraft is off the ground and is seen to be climbing away from the airport, control will be handed over to the area control center. The departure controller will give the pilot approval to enter the runway in order to line up and eventually to start the takeoff run. Information on the wind speed and direction will also be given at this time. For example, "Speedbird 11 cleared takeoff 09 right wind 120 at 10."

Left: *Birmingham Visual Control Room.* NATS

Below Left: *Shanwick Operations Room.* NATS

Below: *Aberdeen Approach Control.* NATS

Arrivals

The responsibility for aircraft which are arriving at Heathrow is that of the arrivals controller who deals with landing flights from several miles out from the airfield. The aircraft will approach at a three-degree descent, using the ILS radio beams to line up correctly on the runway centerline. The localizer beam indicates the centerline and the glide slope ensures that the aircraft is at the correct descent angle. A series of approach lights and runway lights also guide the pilot visually. The controller will, be monitoring all arrivals and will not normally issue a landing clearance until the previous aircraft is clear of the runway. Once this is achieved, the arriving flight will be cleared to land. For example, "Alitalia 266 cleared to land 09 left wind 130 at 7." Once the aircraft has safely landed and has vacated the runway, control will be passed back to the ground controller who will then direct the aircraft to its designated gate.

In the same way that departing flights follow Standard Instrument Departure routes, arriving

aircraft also adopt a similar process referred to as Standard Arrival Routes, or STARS. Using Heathrow as an example, there are four arrival positions, two to the north of the airfield and two to the south. These positions are all served by radio navigation beacons and are used to hold aircraft at a particular position during busy periods so that their arrival at the airfield can be sequenced to fit in with the overall traffic pattern. For example, a flight arriving from Frankfurt would normally be cleared to the navigation beacon at Biggin where it would enter the stack at flight level 110, flying in a race-track pattern. Other aircraft also in the stack would be at lower levels awaiting their turn to make an approach to the airport. The lowest level of the stack is flight level 70. The arriving flight would normally be descended 1,000 feet at a time until it reached FL70, at which point it would be directed to leave the stack on a particular radar heading, in readiness for its final approach to the runway.

Details of the airport, including the runways being used and the local weather, are continuously broadcast on a special radio frequency which can be heard by the pilots approaching the London area. This avoids individual controllers having to give these details over the normal voice channels.

Control Centers

Once the flight has left the jurisdiction of the airport controller, the responsibility is handed over to a controller at one of the air traffic control centers who then gives clearance for the aircraft to continue on its journey.

In the U.K., the main ATC center is at West Drayton, a few miles to the north of Heathrow, with a separate center at Manchester which deals with traffic in the north of England up to flight level 275. The West Drayton center covers the whole of England and Wales.

Scotland and Northern Ireland are covered by a center located at Prestwick. The Republic of Ireland has a separate center based at Shannon. The eastern half of the North Atlantic is the responsibility of a center which is also based at Prestwick, operating in conjunction with a high frequency radio station based in Ireland a few miles from Shannon. The

Left: *Air Traffic management; the en route control center in America.* Peter R. March

ATC

callsign used for oceanic traffic is "Shanwick", a combination of the words "Shannon" and "Prestwick."

A new center will soon be opened at Swanwick, near Fareham in Hampshire, to replace West Drayton. This will have very sophisticated facilities enabling a significant increase in the volume of traffic which can be managed. New centers are also being constructed at Prestwick and Shannon. The centers cover all upper airspace, the airways system, and terminal areas. The area of responsibility is sub-divided into blocks of airspace, referred to as sectors, each with a team of controllers and specific radio frequencies. Some sectors are also split vertically with different controllers taking responsibility for traffic at different levels.

Left: *A view of Swanwick*. Graham Duke

Below Left: *The ATC College, Bournemouth*. Graham Duke

Below: *Manchester Control Center*. NATS

The information presented to the controller is in the form of a printed strip containing the details of each aircraft and the estimated time of arrival into that particular sector. The strips are arranged in racks alongside the controller in the order in which the aircraft are expected. The controller is also able to see the individual flights on the radar screen, together with their flight levels. Some radar systems also include other information—for example, the destination and the arrival sequence number. The modern trend is to display flight strips electronically on the edge of the radar display.

As the aircraft approaches the particular sector, the pilot will contact the controller on a specified frequency and will then be given a clearance to route through that particular piece of airspace. As the flight progresses through the sector and approaches the edge of the sector, the controller will instruct the pilot to change radio frequency to the next sector team. Similarly, if the aircraft is landing at an airport, the transfer will be to the appropriate airport frequency.

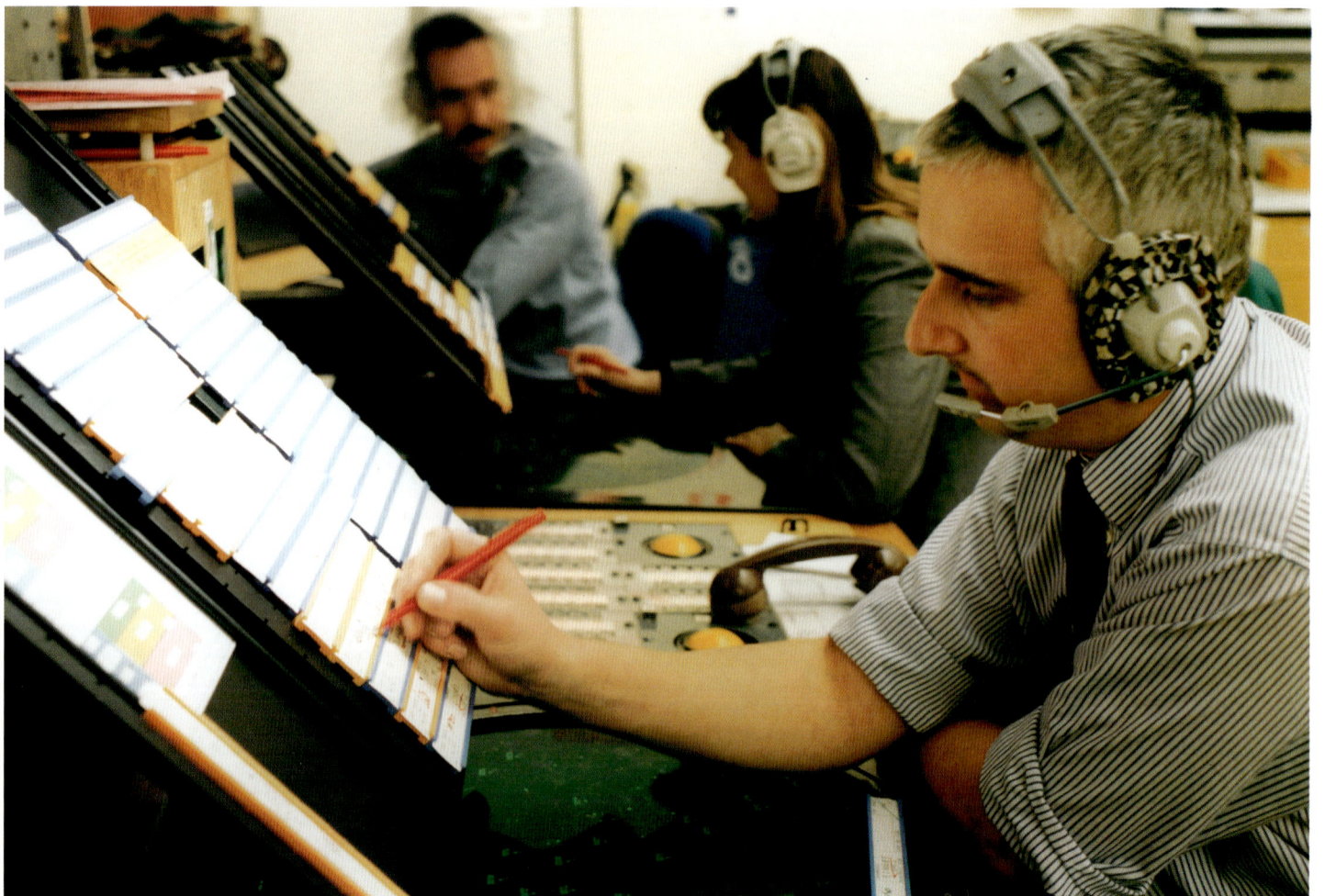

The controller directs the pilot along the route by issuing instructions to climb or descend, to turn to the left or the right, and to increase or decrease speed. In the example used earlier, a typical message following departure would be as follows: "Speedbird 11 good morning, you are identified, climb to flight level 150, after passing flight level 120 route direct to Dover."

One of the essentials of air traffic control is the coordination between the various control teams, and no aircraft is transferred to another controller unless an agreement has been reached on the handover.

Left: *Birmingham Visual Control Room. NATS*

Below Left: *The London and Area Terminal Control Center at West Drayton. NATS*

Below: *The London and Area Terminal Control Center at West Drayton. NATS*

Flights in upper airspace operate at flight levels which comply with an internationally-agreed series of levels depending on the direction of the flight. These are known as "semicircular cruising levels" and are currently separated by 2,000 feet. However, improved height-keeping facilities on aircraft now ensure that very accurate flight levels can be maintained and this has allowed the introduction of reduced vertical separation standards where the 2,000 feet minimum has been reduced to 1,000 feet. This reduction was first implemented over the North Atlantic, where an additional four levels are now available. In the U.K., reduced separation was introduced in April 2001 where an additional six levels were added.

In mainland Europe, reduced separation is planned for introduction in January 2002.

Modern Developments

The major change which can be expected in the coming years is the increasing use of satellite technology and datalink message handling. The present

Above: *The curved radar display positions are clearly shown in this view of the new center at Swanwick.* NATS

Left: *The Terminal Control Room at LATCC.* Airsys ATM

system of passing messages to aircraft by voice is limited both in capacity and flexibility. Trials have been continuing for several years in the transfer of control messages by datalink using satellites where necessary and employing the use of unique identifying codes for separate aircraft. The present system of sending messages means that they are not directed exclusively to one flight, but can be intercepted and acted upon by a flight for which they were not intended. With the latest type of transponder, every aircraft can be given its own identity, meaning that the information can be addressed to that particular flight. It also means that information from the aircraft to the ground is also unique and the chances of error are very much reduced. Instructions to pilots to climb or descend, or to change heading, are issued by datalink and accepted or rejected by the pilot.

A further development is the use of automatic dependent surveillance where transponders on individual aircraft communicate with other flights in the vicinity and are able to resolve possible conflicts automatically. Pilots become aware of other traffic in their region without the involvement of the ground controllers and this will eventually permit pilots to have more of a say in how their individual flight can be conducted. Under this principle, the ground controller becomes an airspace manager monitoring the progress of flights and only intervenes when a conflict appears to be developing.

The overall drive towards improved navigation and reduced separation, both vertically and horizontally, is embraced in the program for Communication, Navigation, Surveillance, and Air Traffic Management (CNS/ATM), and through the "single sky" for Europe concept driven by EURO-CONTROL. The planning of flights will be achieved in four dimensions with crossing points throughout the route being specified within seconds so that conflicts and uneconomic flight profiles can be avoided.

Above Left: *Inside the control tower at Atlanta, GA.* Peter R. March

Left: *While it may not have the traffic movements of Atlanta, local ATC is still vitally important to maintain safety. This is the control tower at Filton, Bristol.* Peter R. March

Right: *Luxembourg airport air traffic control tower.* Peter R. March

Part 5

The Journey

Preparation

When most passengers plan to take a journey by aircraft, whether it is a local domestic service or a major international flight, the concern is normally to check-in within the appropriate time, travel in reasonable comfort, and arrive at the destination complete with baggage. Few passengers would be expected to give a thought to the fact that planning for the average international or domestic flight to and from a major airport probably started two years before the flight took off. It may be appropriate to take, as an example, a flight from Perth International Airport in Western Australia on a Qantas domestic flight to Sydney, followed by an international flight on what used to be known as part of the Kangaroo Service from Australia to the U.K., from Sydney to Singapore. The ultimate route will be to Frankfurt, with a European connection to London Heathrow.

Except for new routes and services, the planning for regular scheduled operations is a continuous process, but probably the first essential task is to ensure that there is a slot available at the relevant airports. A slot is a time and space allocated at a major airport to allow the arrival of a flight within the normal traffic pattern, and a gate where the airliner can be parked to unload the passengers and cargo and prepare for the next departure. Diplomatic clearances may be required for flying through foreign airspace, particularly if it is a new route, where the airline and government of the countries concerned come to an agreement and grant permission for overflying, usually by a predefined route or established airway.

The slots requested at various destinations are not sought in isolation. Many major international airports are also hubs providing passengers and

Left: *Air transport is booming all over the world at the start of the twenty-first century. The new business means that even smaller airfields are gaining the new infrastructure necessary to deal with extra passengers. This is Bristol Lulsgate from the air showing the new terminal opened in February 2000. Peter R. March*

cargo for other flights. When a Qantas Boeing 747-400 arrives at Singapore, it will normally fly on to its ultimate destination of Sydney, another seven flying hours away. Having flown overnight and through a day from Europe with up to twelve hours in the air, the 747-400 arrives at Singapore at dusk and flies overnight to Sydney, arriving early the next morning. Meanwhile, some passengers and cargo from the European flight will either have disembarked at Singapore or transferred to flights bound for other destinations. Qantas would expect some passengers and payload to travel to other destinations in Australia, as well as on other airlines picking up business for Asian destinations. Qantas would therefore not only need to achieve the slot for the arrival and departure of the Boeing 747-400 at Singapore to match the typical departure slots in

Left: *The airbridge is a mobile access for most airliners arriving at major airports. It is kept parked with the pivoted wheels in a circle. When an airliner taxies along the black-outlined yellow line to the appropriate marked position, an operator maneuvers the access platform within the white-outlined, red-lined area to match up with the passenger forward door at sill height. The steps down to the apron are used by maintenance personnel and the crew member making the pre-flight walk-around inspection.* Philip J. Birtles

Below Left: *For a flight to be permitted into a busy international airport, a slot has to be generated within the overall traffic pattern sometimes two years in advance. Air New Zealand 767-300ER ZK-NCE taxies to the assigned stand on arrival at Sydney International Airport.* Philip J. Birtles

Below: *Canadian 767-300ER C-GLCA on the assigned stand at Sydney International Airport.* Philip J. Birtles

Above: *For passengers who flew from Europe by 747-400 to Singapore, some would have transferred to the smaller Qantas 767-300ER VH-OGR to fly to Perth in Western Australia. This flight is a joint Qantas/BA operation combining the passengers from both airlines in addition to bringing passengers from Singapore either direct or in transit. BA and Qantas have formed a global alliance known as One World, and BA has a 25 percent interest in Qantas.*
Philip J. Birtles

Right: *The Qantas 767-300ER fleet are cleared for Erops— Extended Range Operations, which allows a twin-jet airliner to fly up to 180 minutes from a suitable diversionary airfield when flying on one engine in the unlikely event of a failure. Qantas 767-300ER VH-OGC is ready to depart from Perth to Singapore where even over land there are few available airports en route and Erops conditions apply.*
Philip J. Birtles

The Journey

Europe, which are often subject to night curfews, but they would also have to negotiate additional slots for flights in smaller capacity airliners to other places in Australia. Examples include a direct flight to Perth in conjunction with their One World partner British Airways (BA), where both Qantas and BA flight numbers are assigned to one flight, avoiding wasteful capacity duplication, and possibly Adelaide, Melbourne, Darwin, and Brisbane in other parts of Australia.

The operators must have the airliners' availability to maintain these services, not only in terms of overall aircraft in the fleet size ordered from the manufacturers, but also allowing for maintenance, both scheduled and unscheduled, and overall capacity for passengers and cargo. For the longer routes, aircraft with sufficient range or endurance must be assigned, with payload capacity a major consideration. If there are to be long overwater or remote overland routes to be flown, the airliner must have more than two engines, unless a twin-engine aircraft has approval and proven systems integrity for long-range flights. This is often the case with modern Airbus and Boeing airliners where a twin-engine aircraft is more appropriate to the capacity required for a less busy destination.

At least a year in advance of a flight, the airline sales organization will start selling seats and cargo space. Catering requirements will be determined to take into account special dietary needs of different nationalities, particularly those from stops along the route where flights from other countries may be connecting for the ultimate destination. Three to six months before the flight is scheduled, if the reservations are not reaching the expected levels, the marketing and sales organizations will consider some special promotions based on the predicted sales forecast. The important criteria is yield management to ensure the maximum utilization of the space on the aircraft for passengers and cargo. Depending on the expected sales, the size of the aircraft can be downgraded or upgraded and the seat

Above Left: *Not all slot assignments are in isolation. The arrival of a Qantas 747-400 could have carried passengers for other destinations which may be served by Qantas 767-300ER VH-OGH at Sydney International Terminal.* Philip J. Birtles

Left: *For any engineering work, whether overnight check and configuration changes, or heavy maintenance, the aircraft is normally pulled into the hangar where it is surrounded by custom-built staging for full access. BA Boeing 777-200 G-VIID is pulled in the Heathrow Engineering base for overnight maintenance.* Philip J. Birtles

Right: *The aft galley of the Airbus A340 is a fixed installation, but the similar units in the mid-cabin areas can be relocated according to the passenger configuration.* Philip J. Birtles

Overleaf: *Many operators use promotional color schemes to help market the airline, although it is not always easy to see them due to airport security and difficult access. Thai A330 HS-TEK at Perth has been painted to show a dragon boat with many oarsmen to promote tourism to Thailand.* Philip J. Birtles

configuration can be altered to match the sales being achieved. A particular example is the movement of the boundary between the business-class cabin and the economy class, although first class remains fixed in most cases. Modern airliners have the capability of a wide variation in cabin layout, with toilets and galleys capable of being moved to new positions during an overnight stop to ensure

Left: *When a modern two-crew airliner such as the 747-400 is expected to fly over a long-haul route taking the flight crew duty in excess of twelve hours, an additional "light" crew is carried to fly the middle section of the flight while the "heavy" crew are able to rest. The heavy captain, Captain Paul Grenet (third from left) carries out the briefing of the double crew before departure from Heathrow on a flight to Singapore. Philip J. Birtles*

Below Left: *The flight engineers panel of a Lockheed TriStar showing the complexity of the systems management now looked after by the two pilots and computers in the modern Efis cockpit. This panel also has the addition of a small video screen on the bottom right, as it has been modified into a flight refueling tanker for the RAF. Philip J. Birtles*

Below: *The two-crew flight deck of the Boeing 747-400 with the captain's PFD on the left and the ND beside it. The EICAS displays are in the center and monitor systems performance similar to the duties formerly undertaken by the flight engineer. Philip J. Birtles*

the most efficient use of the aircraft. If seats are still expected to be available in the month before departure, further promotions are offered to at least sell the seats for just above cost, often to staff members of the airline and their families. As a result, an economy passenger who paid full fare could be sitting next to someone who has paid perhaps only a third of the regular fare. The airlines and manufacturers are now considering producing a fourth class, giving more room to full-fare economy passengers and allocating the current economy seats and pitch to the low-yield tickets.

Sitting on airliners for long periods is considered bad for the health, particularly in the cramped economy-class seats where deep vein thrombosis (DVT) can cause potential fatal blood clots when a person does not exercise for long periods. It has been suggested that walking machines should be introduced in aircraft cabins, but these would take up a significant amount of space otherwise allocated to passenger seats to make a practical difference. Airbus are looking at the possibility of lower deck toilets, which would not only free up additional space on

the main deck, but give passengers the additional exercise of walking up and down some stairs, as well as along the aisles. DVT is estimated to affect up to 30,000 people a year and at least 800 lawsuits are on hand claiming damages from the airlines. A number of major airlines are considering preventive action, with the recommendation that passengers wear loose clothing, eat light meals and limit the consumption of alcohol to reduce the risk of DVT. In some of the airline flight magazines, advice is given about how to exercise while remaining seated. The Qantas Inflight Workout includes foot exercises, knee lifts, neck rolls, knee to chest, forward flex, and shoulder rolls. The exercises should be done for a few minutes every hour, in addition to walking along the aisles, and are designed to increase blood circulation.

In addition to aircraft availability, there has to be sufficient flight deck and cabin crew personnel on call to operate the flight safely and according to international law. In the past, the aircrew might consist of the captain sitting in the left-hand seat on the flight deck with the first officer on the right. Behind the captain, the navigator was located at a table with all his instruments to ensure a timely arrival at each airport. Behind the first officer, the flight engineer would monitor the operation of the aircraft systems, including pressurization, air conditioning, fuel flows, efficient engine operation, electrical, and hydraulic systems. With the advent of improved navigation systems worldwide and satellites giving precise inertial navigation information, the navigator was made unnecessary in the late 1950s and early 1960s as the older aircraft were phased out of service. In the 1980s, the flight engineer became obsolete with the computerized

Above Left: *When the useful life of a passenger airliner is over, many are converted to pure cargo configuration for operation by specialist airlines. The TriStar has been one of the examples of the older wide-body airliners used for bulky loads over long ranges. The cargo conversation consists of providing an upward-opening door in the passenger cabin and removing all the passenger services, including blocking off the windows. A cargo handling system is installed to allow handling and stowage of the load on the main deck.* Philip J. Birtles

Left: *After use by the initial operator who acquired the airliner new, the aircraft are often passed on to charter operators who take advantage of the low capital cost until maintenance costs become uneconomical. Lockheed TriStar G-BBAF flew its last operation with BA and was used by Caledonian for holiday charter work, and is seen about to land at Rhodes in September 1995.* Philip J. Birtles

The Journey

cockpits allowing safe and efficient operation by two pilots on all but the longest routes. Where a flight is scheduled to have a crew duty operation exceeding twelve hours, an additional light crew is carried to operate the aircraft during the middle part of the flight, allowing the takeoff and landing crew to have an adequate rest period.

Some of the second-generation jet airliners are still in regular operation with a crew of three,

Left: *The modern flight simulators are extremely realistic in operation including visual images of approaches to typical airports encountered on the regular airline routes. The simulator is used regularly to ensure the crew is operating with the correct procedures and emergencies can be reproduced realistically without risk to a real airliner. A crew can also ensure that they remain current on the airliner type if it has not been possible to fly the aircraft within the past thirty days. This Rediffusion flight simulator represents the BA Boeing 747-400 flight deck with all the systems reproduced.* Philip J. Birtles

Below Left: *The cabin crew is responsible for passenger safety as well as cabin service. On international flights, they will represent the major national destinations being served with a range of language skills.* Philip J. Birtles

Below: *Catering being loaded aboard Singapore Airlines 777-300ER 9V-SQC at Perth International Airport through the port door adjacent to the business-class cabin.* Philip J. Birtles

including a flight engineer, but many of these are either being retired or converted into their third life as pure cargo aircraft. Each airliner has at least two lives, the first one with the airline which ordered and defined the specifications when the aircraft was newly built. The second life is with a secondary international, domestic, or charter operator who often operates under lease at a low capital cost, but as the aircraft becomes older, the running and maintenance costs increase until the aircraft is no longer viable. This can often be caused by the lack of spare parts, high fuel consumption, or more commonly the engine noise exceeding internationally-agreed levels.

The flight and cabin crew have to be assigned to the flight and it is essential that they work well as a team as well as individuals. They need to be correctly licensed with medical examinations updated and need to be qualified on the aircraft type and familiar with its operation. If the captain has not flown the type within the previous thirty days, he will need to have a test-run in the appropriate simulator to ensure that he is entirely familiar with the operation and safety procedures. On short flights

Right: *Passenger baggage in containers and cargo on covered pallets being loaded aboard wide-body Qantas 767-200ER VH-ZXE at the Perth Domestic Terminal.* Philip J. Birtles

this is rarely a problem, as the captain and first officer are able to maintain practice during their normal daily activities. Even for crews maintaining flying currency, there can be three four-hour sessions booked on the simulator to ensure correct procedures and the capability of dealing with emergencies. There will also be an annual line-check, when a training captain will monitor crew performance in the operating environment.

It can be very different with long-haul crews, as on a flight, whatever the duration, there is only one

Left: *Passenger baggage and freight being loaded in containers into the aft hold of Ansett 767-200ER VH-RMF at the Perth Domestic Terminal.* Philip J. Birtles

Below Left: *Engineering support is provided by the airline staff at the home base, and also for visiting operators where it is not economical to do it for themselves.* Philip J. Birtles

Below: *The modern turbofan engines are so large that an engineer can step inside the intake to inspect the front end for any damage.* Philip J. Birtles

takeoff and landing; where on short-haul services the crew may achieve two or three rotations in a duty day, the long-haul crew may make only one landing after a twelve-hour flight. Although most modern airliners are equipped for automatic landing, the pilots like to keep current with manual landings, and the captain needs to share the experience with the first officer. Only the primary heavy operating crew obtains the experience of takeoff and landing, while the relief light crew has to be content with operating the aircraft during the cruise. Although manual landings are usually preferred by the crews, it is necessary to make automatic landings from time to time to maintain an awareness of the correct procedures. A long-haul pilot therefore can have difficulty remaining current on the aircraft type and could need a day on the simulator to be qualified to operate the aircraft. Both air and ground crews are rostered for each flight, particularly on long international routes, but they do not remain together as a team, unlike domestic flights which will probably be operated by

the same flight crew throughout a duty period, but with different cabin crews. The crews for domestic flights could be away from home for up to five days, while long-range international flight and cabin crews could be away from home for up to ten days. Normal duty times are up to twelve hours, with some exceptions to fourteen hours, with corresponding time off. After an overall duty period of ten days, the crew member would expect to be off duty for about five days. Not all crew members live close to the base airport, and a longer time spent off-duty is often desirable.

The cabin crew's primary function is to ensure the safety of the passengers, particularly if there is any form of emergency. Usually, the only sign of this function is the safety briefing at the start of every flight, but they are normally qualified in the basic care of sick or ill passengers and looking after those

Below: The ground engineer checks the oil levels in an engine of a Boeing 767-300 at London Gatwick. Philip J. Birtles

Right: When refueling at major airports, the fuel is usually metered by a special vehicle from underground pipes and tanks. A connection is made with the access point close to the aircraft with a high-visibility marked hose, and the fuel is pumped under pressure through a single point under the wing leading edge. Fuel and catering is being serviced for Malaysia 777-300ER 9M-MRK at Perth. Philip J. Birtles

with special needs such as disabilities or young families. The cabin crew is usually chosen for communications abilities in the languages of the passengers expected on the flight, taking into account the departure and arrival points. As an additional important function, the cabin crew attends to the comforts of the passengers, providing appropriate refreshments throughout the flight. The cabin crew is responsible for delivering the "Product," which is the level of service, and is essential for maintaining the loyalty of airline customers in a highly competitive market. The products themselves can take up to two years to develop and include such features as seats reclining into beds in first class and some upper business class, and seat-back entertainment systems in economy class.

Although alcohol is often freely available on many flights, it leads to dehydration, particularly on long flights, and according to international air law, it is illegal to be intoxicated on board an aircraft. There have been a number of occasions when passengers have been refused permission to board due to the influence of alcohol and their baggage removed until they sober up enough for a later flight. It is not unknown for a captain to divert to an alternative airfield to have drunken passengers removed as undesirable to have on board and posing a safety risk to the other passengers.

The flight and cabin crews, except for some short-haul feeder operations, can rarely be expected to be operating from their home base every night. Duty hours and efficient operations often dictate prolonged periods away from home, particularly with long-haul operations and the airline therefore

Left: Some of the older aircraft are still powered by piston engines, although most are now turbine powered and fueled by kerosene. This vehicle delivers Aviation Gasoline to piston engine aircraft. Philip J. Birtles

Below Left: Not all aircraft are located close to the fuel main system, and this mobile fuel tanker was available to provide fuel to a trio of RAAF C-130H Hercules visiting Perth as the nearby Pearce Air Force Base was closed for routine maintenance. Philip J. Birtles

Below: Fuel has to be continually supplied to the underground storage tanks and this Mobil tanker is ready to deliver a load of Jet A-1 fuel for the domestic terminal at Perth. Philip J. Birtles

Below: *A Learjet 610 awaits departure.* Peter R. March

The Journey

make permanent long-term bookings in hotels close to the airport for a hundred or more crew members, whether the rooms are used or not. These rooms are available around the clock, as the crews need the rest when they arrive, and not necessarily at local bedtime. On long-range services, crews may be assigned to fly some services from a regional hub, such as Singapore, where they would have time to adjust to the local time zones. When a Boeing 747 arrives at Singapore, the crew is replaced for the next leg, and therefore after a suitable rest period, they could fly a service to a more distant destina-

Left: *Fuel spillage is a constant hazard on airport aprons, and when it happens efforts have to be made to clear it up. A solution of water and slurry is poured over the domestic apron at Perth and a brush-equipped tractor clears the liquid.* Philip J. Birtles

Below Left: *At all major airports, safety and security vehicles ensure that the airport environment is safe for operations. Due to being refueled overnight for a departure early in the morning, when the departure was delayed, the heat of Western Australia soon expanded the fuel and caused a spill, which is being monitored by the airport safety staff.* Philip J. Birtles

Below: *At Sydney International Airport, the safety and security staff maintain a close liaison with the spill response team.* Philip J. Birtles

tion, using the hub as the base for a period. In addition to the appropriate duty time, rest period and accommodation, the crews need transportation to and from the hotel and financial allowances to cover expenses while away from home. Some passengers may find air travel tiring, but the flight crew has to remain alert the whole time, and the cabin crew is on duty throughout the duration of the flight, with some rest periods during lulls on long flights. Although the cabin crew is able to move about the cabin, dehydration is a constant problem for those on continuous operations over a period of time.

In addition to the flight and cabin crews, a whole range of other people are essential to the safe and timely operation of an airliner once it appears at the departure gate. While an airliner is on turnaround the cabin has to be cleaned and a check made to ensure that all the safety equipment is on board and functional. For an international journey, sufficient check-in staff need to be available at least three hours in advance of departure, with more coming on duty as the number of passengers builds up to a peak about two hours before departure. By this time, the catering organization should have had all

Above: *All major regional and international airports will have their own meteorology organization complete with satellite link to provide the departing airliners with an en route weather forecast. The Australian Government Bureau of Meteorology at Perth International Airport is located in a modern complex inside the airport boundary, having previously occupied the old control tower.* Philip J. Birtles

Left: *In the event of an emergency, all airports keep a fire and rescue service available during the period of operation. The highly trained and constantly alert crews are dedicated to aircraft incidents and do not deal with domestic airport fires. The fire station at Perth has an elevated control room at one end and is located in front of the now-empty old control tower.* Philip J. Birtles

the bookings for special diets, including children's meals, but there are always passengers who have forgotten to make known their special requirements when booking, and in anticipation of this, additional special meals are often prepared in advance. While every effort is made to sit families and passengers who are traveling together close to each other, difficulties can occur if reservations have been made separately. Most of the passenger seat assignments are made twenty-four hours before the flight

Left: With the large loads of cargo and baggage which can be put aboard the modern wide-body jet airliner, substantial lifting vehicles and transport trailers are required. Cathay Pacific A330 B-HLA is being prepared for departure from Perth International Airport, bound for Hong Kong. Philip J. Birtles

Below Left: The trailers which are used to bring the pallets and containers to the aircraft are equipped with rollers to allow the loads to be manhandled without mechanical aids onto the loading platform ready for loading aboard Qantas 767-300ER VH-OGJ at Perth. Philip J. Birtles

Below: Once the containers or pallets are pushed on to the loading vehicle, the base is raised to the aircraft cargo hold sill level and driven on board by mechanical rollers. This Qantas 767-300ER VH-OGJ is being prepared for departure at Perth. Philip J. Birtles

is due to depart, including those passengers who have requested a particular location. Fortunately, cigarette smoking is banned on most flights, which not only avoids the discomfort of a non-smoker being seated in a smoking area, but also keeps the cabin and air conditioning system much cleaner. Check-in for domestic flights is usually an hour prior to departure, since the passenger and cargo loads are often less, and the catering is simpler. There are also less formalities for the preparation of the flight.

Although many regular passengers travel reasonably light and do not take long to check-in, other passengers, such as a large family, may turn up with two or three carts loaded with baggage, adding extra weight to the load in the underfloor hold. This gives an extra challenge to the people responsible for calculating the loading of the aircraft. Security and safety is of paramount importance to the airlines and there are a number of items which cannot be carried on an aircraft, and others which require special permission. Among the latter category are guns, which are handled specially with ammunition

Right: *Containers and pallets are brought out to Singapore Airlines 777-30ER 9V-SQC and are lifted aboard into both the front and rear holds.*
Philip J. Birtles

Above: *Many of the bulk pallets are covered by metal cases and have been packed in a warehouse off the airport.* Philip J. Birtles

Right: *Some cargo is packed in full hold width freight containers, maneuvered off the delivery trolley by mechanical means and raised on the loading platform into the hold of the Japan Airlines 777-300ER JA8984 at Tokyo.* Philip J. Birtles

The Journey

packed separately. Obviously, explosives—including fireworks—are banned, as well as wet-cell batteries, magnetized materials, compressed gases, drugs, and often plant life. Anything containing mercury is undesirable, as should it break, the material is highly corrosive to aluminium structures.

At many airports, all check in baggage is screened during the journey through the baggage system, each item being identified by a computer bar code and a three-letter destination code. At

Left: Qantas 767-300ER VH-OGC is having the final cargo and baggage loaded and catering put on board in the rear vestibule at Perth. Philip J. Birtles

Below Left: While catering is being loaded through both access doors to the rear vestibule in Singapore 777-300ER 9V-SQG at Perth, the baggage and cargo train load is being taken aboard with a number of large pallets secured by netting. Philip J. Birtles

Below: The "boot" on a modern wide-body jet airliner is at the tail end and used for awkwardly-sized items of baggage which have to be loaded by hand up a mobile conveyor, as in this Qantas 767-300ER VH-OGJ at Perth. Philip J. Birtles

other airports the baggage may be screened at regular intervals, but there are few modern airports which do not perform some type of baggage security. Regular passengers are also familiar with the usual passenger and hand baggage security checks, which require a team of five or six people on each entry point to maintain a reasonable flow of passengers. This security check is a thankless but essential task, with turns being taken by the security staff on the monitor screen to maintain alertness, and at least one male and female to undertake the necessary body search if alerted by the metal detector, although the hand-held metal detector is probably the most efficient detection device for body searches. Sufficient security staff need to be on duty to ensure that there are no delays to passengers even at the peak times.

Sufficient engineering and handling staff need to be on duty to provide maintenance support during a turnaround between arrival and departure. If the arriving crew reports any problems with the aircraft, a decision needs to be made as to whether a repair needs to be done before the next flight, or

Below: *With loading completed, the rear cargo door and the boot are closed, ready for Japan Airlines 777-300ER JA8984 to depart from Tokyo.* Philip J. Birtles

Above: *The ground crew prepares for the push back of Japan Airlines 777-300ER JA8984 at Tokyo.*
Philip J. Birtles

Left: *As the tug pushes back Japan Airlines 777-300ER JA8984 at Tokyo it passes a pair of airbridges used to board passengers through two entry doors on the port side. The nearest one would have been used for passengers in the first-class cabin.*
Philip J. Birtles

whether it can wait until the next maintenance check is due. Once again, safety is the deciding factor, but also efficient performance is taken into account.

Obviously, refueling is often carried out, unless the aircraft is operating on a number of short-haul sectors, but a visual check is always made of the contents. Fuel is normally carried in integral tanks in the wings, with additional capacity in the wing center section under the cabin. The wing structure is

Left: *While the wide-body airliners can carry cargo and baggage in standard containers, the narrow-body airliners like this Qantas 737-300 VH-TAJ have to be loaded manually with individual items carried up mobile conveyor belts.* Philip J. Birtles

Below Left: *To save on handling costs, some airliners are equipped with integral airstairs. This Aero Lloyd MD-83 D-ALLQ is seen at Rhodes for a holiday charter in September 2000 with self-contained airstairs at the front door and underneath the rear fuselage.* Philip J. Birtles

Below: *Some airlines order what are known as Combis, which are adaptations of mainly wide-body airliners with an upward-opening cargo door in the rear cabin to allow cargo containers to be carried on the main deck. This Air France 747-400 F-GISE is a combi version and is awaiting clearance for takeoff from Hong Kong Kai Tak in April 1998.* Philip J. Birtles

literally sealed to contain the fuel with no separate tanks, and fuel pumps and pipes manage the flow throughout the flight to maintain the aircraft in balance and reduce bending loads on the structure. Where very long range is required additional fuel can be located on the vertical tailfin, horizontal tailplane or in additional tanks in the cargo hold, usually close to the wing center section. At most modern airports, fuel is supplied from underground pipes and metered out by a special vehicle which delivers the fuel under pressure through a single point under the wing's leading edge. A system of cross-feed valves ensure that the fuel is distributed evenly across the aircraft. The ground crew is also responsible for checking various other consumables such as engine oil and hydraulic fluid, as well as checking for any leaks or damage to the engines or airframe, perhaps caused by bird strikes at lower levels on takeoff or approach. Engine oil filters are checked, and magnetic detectors are used to determine if there is any internal damage to the bearings and other working parts of the engine. A modern fan-jet engine should be able to continue in operation for many years without removal from the wing, but from time to time, modules may need changing

Below: Toilet emptying on a Continental Express Brasilia. Peter R. March

The Journey

when they become faulty. The condition of the tires will be checked, and if damage has occurred, the wheels and brakes will also be inspected to help determine the cause of the tire damage. Although wing flaps and reverse thrust are usually employed during landing to avoid wear and tear, the brakes can often become hot, and until they have cooled down to an acceptable temperature, the aircraft cannot depart. This can be a restriction on short-haul operations, but is rarely a problem for long

flights, which experience longer turnarounds. One of the major safety tests for an airliner to achieve a certificate of airworthiness is a maximum energy stop after landing at the heaviest allowable weight. The brakes can become red-hot and the tires often burst with flames coming from the wheels. This condition has to be maintained safely for ten minutes, giving fire vehicles sufficient time to arrive and put out the fire. Although aircraft brakes used to be made from steel, they are now made from carbon composite, which not only saves a considerable amount of weight, but also absorbs heat more effectively and cools faster.

While the airline's own staff will probably be responsible for the handling at the main bases, any overseas destinations would normally be contracted out to the local major international operator, or an airline with similar aircraft. In return, the home-based airline would undertake the handling under contract for visiting aircraft. For example at Perth International Airport, Ansett handles Air Mauritius and Malaysia flights, while Qantas handles the remainder of the international flights. This avoids employing a large number of extra people for perhaps only one daily

Left: *Not all journeys start from major airports. Passengers are fed to the main airport from outlying areas by various commuter aircraft. This Eastern Australia Dash-7 VH-TQO provides an exclusive low-cost feeder service to Qantas at Sydney and is painted in the colors of the major airline.* Philip J. Birtles

Below Left: *Among the regional jet aircraft gradually replacing the older prop-jet commuter types is the popular Brazilian Embraer EMB-145. This BA Regional Airlines example G-EMBN is operating feeder services from Manchester International Airport.* Philip J. Birtles

Below: *ASA operates Bombadier RJ jets on behalf of Delta Air Lines from Atlanta International Airport. This Delta Connection RJ N849AS is painted to commemorate twenty years of working with Delta and is waiting in the takeoff line at Atlanta in May 2000.* Philip J. Birtles

AIRPORT

Below: *National Jet Systems operates a fleet of BAe 146 four fan-jet engine airliners as Airlink on feeder services for Qantas. BAe 146-200 VH-NJJ is boarding the final passengers via normal steps before push-back and departure. The aircraft is painted in Qantas colors and the NJS cabin crew wears Qantas uniforms.* Philip J. Birtles

Left: *Airtours 737 seen from new terminal at Lulsgate.* Peter R. March

Below Left and Right: *Tax-free shopping has always been one of the great perks of international travel. Here, tax-free items are on sale at Terminal 2, Heathrow.* Peter R. March

Below: *As has been seen only too often, without strict controls air transport can become very dangerous. The filtering of passengers through baggage and personal checks is essential for air safety and immigration control. This is passport control at Terminal 2, Heathrow.* Peter R. March

flight, together with the costs of purchasing specialized equipment which would be underutilized.

When an airliner arrives on the stand, while the first passengers are disembarking, a fleet of special vehicles and equipment surrounds the aircraft. With the passengers disembarking on the left-hand side, or port side, through the forward section of the aircraft via an airbridge, the special cargo-handling equipment approaches the freight hold access doors on the right, or starboard side. This avoids conflict of equipment and people, and in some cases passengers also disembark at the rear, either down airstairs on the port side or an airstair ramp underneath the tail. The most common examples of the latter are the Boeing 727 and McDonnell Douglas DC-9/MD-80 family of airliners. In some cases, particularly on low-cost charter flights, the aircraft can be fitted with retractable airstairs to reduce handling costs and give greater independence at outstations.

In the forward and rear cargo holds of wide-bodied jet airliners, baggage and freight is often packed under the cabin floors in standard containers, which, when put side-by side, can usually be loaded as a pair into the aircraft hold. More bulky items can be put on standard pallets and secured by nets or covered by an aluminium igloo. In addition to the regular passenger baggage, the cargo hold could contain high-value consumer and manufactured goods and perishable goods such as fruit and vegetables and livestock such as live lobsters. Most airliners are configured with an animal bay for the carriage of passengers' pets, which need to arrive in good condition without undue stress. At the extreme rear of the aircraft is Hold 5, or the "boot," where awkwardly-sized and shaped baggage and cargo can be loaded manually.

When the passengers check-in, if they are flying first-class, the baggage is put into a priority container to ensure an early delivery at the destination.

Above Left: Qantas 737-4L7 c/n 26961 VH-TJW arrives at the domestic terminal at Perth International Airport in January 2001. This aircraft was originally delivered to Air Nauru, but acquired by Qantas in June 1995. Philip J. Birtles

Left: The Qantas 737-400 eases forward and stops to match the passenger exit door with the airbridge. Philip J. Birtles

A service container is also reserved for crew baggage and any excess priority luggage. In many cases of international flights, there will also be a diplomatic locker for high-value items and sensitive documents with restricted access to the station managers at the various destinations. The regular under-floor holds are numbered one to four, the divisions being on either side of the access door. There are numbered positions for the containers and cargo pallets, the pallets often having been preloaded in advance at bonded warehouses outside the airport. Each container and pallet is weighed to the nearest kilogram and the weight is distributed precisely to ensure the correct and safe balance of the aircraft. The writer has been on a Boeing 767-300ER taxiing for departure at Atlanta, when the captain announced that he had been requested to return to the stand. Apparently, the loading control staff had detected an error in the load sheet and required the aircraft to return for the cargo to be moved around to correct the balance. If an aircraft is not fully loaded with passengers, those on board will be distributed to maintain the safe balance. The planning by the load controller begins twenty-four hours before the departure of the flight, and continues until the cargo doors are closed after all the passengers are on board. The passenger check in desk is usually closed thirty minutes before departure to allow the load controller to make the final calculations to maintain the balance of the aircraft within the limits of the center of gravity, which is around the center of the lift of the wings.

Special servicing vehicles ensure that the toilet waste is removed and water is put on board, the access points being under the fuselage and tail to avoid conflict with other service vehicles. The cargo and baggage containers and pallets are towed out by a tug in a long train of roller trailers, and if brought out at once it always looks as if there is too much to fit in the aircraft. However, the cargo vanishes into the holds in a predetermined order, lifted up by special platforms and rolled on board and into the correct position in the hold. The containers and pallets are carefully located to avoid damage to the interior of the aircraft and securely fixed down to avoid any movement in-flight. Some of the larger wide-body jet airliners are configured as combis and have a large additional upward opening cargo door located on the port side of the rear cabin to allow

extra cargo to be loaded on the upper deck behind the passengers. This configuration is commonly used on long, thin routes where the passenger yield is often low, and freight can make up the balance of the weight. The prime economic consideration is always the yield management, which determines which type of aircraft is used for a particular flight, as well as its configuration.

While the aircraft is being refueled, cleaned, and the holds loaded with cargo, the galleys are being cleared from the previous flight, and as is the case in Australia, all perishable material is loaded into special containers for destruction to avoid bringing any plant disease into the country. Once the old catering is removed, the new catering is put on board, with special scissor jack vehicles being used to ensure a compatibility with the aircraft floor height. The catering containers can then be rolled off and on with ease, each trolley being numbered according to its function and location. Alcohol is delivered from the warehouse for consumption on board and also for duty free sales where appropriate. Only unopened bottles can be returned to the warehouse, which is why many airlines use minatures for alcohol, except in first class and sometimes business class, where full bottles of wine are offered. Ovens are fitted into the galleys for the heating of meals as required. The catering access on most airliners is through the access doors on the starboard side opposite to the passenger vestibules at the front and rear of the cabins, and clear of the cargo doors to avoid conflict of access space.

Left: Even before the airbridge canopy is in place and the door opens, the first passenger luggage is moving down the mobile conveyor belt to be loaded on trolleys. Philip J. Birtles

Below Left: With the passenger baggage unloaded, the toilet waste is cleared by the special vehicle under the nose of the aircraft, and catering is being removed from the rear vestibule. Philip J. Birtles

Below: Continental Airlines is based at Houston, TX and is in the top ten of U.S. airlines. Here one of its many 737s taxies past an ATR42x. Peter R. March

Not all journeys start from a major city with an international airport. In some areas of the world, a journey could start from a remote location served typically by a twin-engine prop-jet airliner with perhaps a dozen seats. In this case there are no containers to load, the baggage and freight being loaded by hand into whatever space is made available. From larger regional airports requiring aircraft with fifty or more seats, there is a move from the traditional economic prop-jet airliner to the new regional jet airliners of the type produced by Bombardier in Canada, Fairchild/Dornier and Embraer in Brazil. They are usually flown by a crew of two with a minimum of flight attendants, since exotic catering is rarely included. Many of these regional aircraft are flown by specialized small airlines with lower overheads and operating costs than the major airlines, but they are usually contracted to supply certain levels of service. Sometimes the regional operators are owned by the major airlines which they serve, but retain the original lower-cost independent management structure to maintain economic services. The regional operator may boost its public image with the aircraft painted in the major airline's colors, and the crews wear appropriate uniforms to maintain a seamless image throughout the journey. Qantas, for example, has contracted National Jet Systems (NJS) to operate BAe 146 four-jet airliners on appropriate domestic and short-haul international services. Although the aircraft are owned and maintained by NJS, and the flight and cabin crews are employees of NJS, the aircraft are painted in Qantas colors and the crews wear Qantas uniforms.

Left: *As a tractor tows back another trailer for the cargo, refueling starts.* Philip J. Birtles

Below Left: *With the passenger baggage unloaded, the toilet waste is cleared by the special vehicle under the nose of the aircraft, and catering is being removed from the rear vestibule. Catering is also changed in the forward galley.* Philip J. Birtles

Below: *While the refueling continues and the catering is loaded, the passenger baggage load is split into two to maintain the balance of the aircraft.* Philip J. Birtles

Above Left: *Airbridge attached to Northwest 747-200, Detroit, MI.* Peter R. March

Left: *Busy terminal at Schipol, Amsterdam as Lufthansa and British Midland 737 short-range aircraft are resupplied before another flight.* Brian S. Strickland

Above: *Chartered airlines dominate the short and medium-haul summer markets with holiday traffic. Airtours International was founded in the early 1990s and today serves holiday destinations all over Europe and the Mediterranean. Here, passengers embark on an Airtours A320 for return to London from Alicante, Spain.* Peter R. March

The Trip

With much of the preparation complete, the journey is ready to start. The aircraft may be starting from the airline's main base, in which case it is brought to the stand about one hour before departure to avoid incurring high airport fees for parking longer than necessary in a prime position. If the aircraft is away from base, it may have flown in on a previous schedule an hour earlier, and either the crew has enough duty time to take it to the next destination, or a new crew is assigned. If it is an early-morning flight, the aircraft may have been on the stand overnight, ready for the next departure. If it is the first flight of the day, the aircraft will have had its daily inspection to ensure all the vital systems are operating appropriately for the flight.

The check-in desk is open early, and when I arrive at the Qantas domestic terminal at Perth Airport, I am able to select an aisle seat to allow easy access to the flight deck when appropriate. My flight from Sydney to Perth before Christmas had been in a Qantas 767-200, so it was natural to expect a similar aircraft for the journey back to Sydney. When I settled into the departure/arrival lounge at Gate 1, there was a 737-300 being prepared for departure to Melbourne, and Gates 2 and 3 were empty. My flight, QF 642 for Sydney, was not due to depart until 9:00 a.m., and the inbound flight was due at 8:00 a.m. As I settled down to wait, the passengers loaded on to the Melbourne-bound flight and it was soon ready for push-back. Just before 8:00 a.m., another 737 landed on runway 03, and made its way to Gate 2 where I was waiting. It turned out to be a Qantas 737-400 VH-TJW demonstrating effective yield management, since a 767-200 would have had more capacity than

Left: *With the loading completed, Qantas 737-400 VH-TJG is pushed back from the Sydney Domestic Terminal and the ground crew member has just disconnected the radio link to signal to the captain that the aircraft is ready for departure.* Philip J. Birtles

Above Left: *Qantas 737-400 VH-TJA departs from Sydney on another domestic flight.* Philip J. Birtles

Far Left: *Captain Bruce Maskeill in the left-hand seat of 737-400 VH-TJW during the cruise with the twin Efis displays in front, one above the other.* Philip J. Birtles

Left: *The approach is made to Runway 34L at Sydney, which is partly built on reclaimed land into Botany Bay. The International Terminal is on the left and the Domestic on the right.* Philip J. Birtles

Below: *The 737-400 is coming in over the threshold as a 747-400 taxies out to the holding point for the same runway.* Philip J. Birtles

required for this early Monday morning service to Sydney. There was no delay in the passengers disembarking, and the baggage was rapidly unloaded, followed by the arrival of the refueling wagon. Although considerably smaller than a Jumbo Jet, the refueler was present for almost the entire hour on the ground, as the fuel has to be metered into the wings gradually to avoid pressure surge and possibly airlocks. The toilet waste vehicle clears the tanks under the nose and then the tail, and new toilet fluid is pumped aboard. Not long after the incoming baggage and cargo has been unloaded by hand onto mobile belts, the next load for the departing flight is being pulled out with a careful balance being maintained between the forward and rear holds. Loading cannot be so precise when the baggage and freight is loose, but the safe balance of the aircraft is still maintained.

While the passengers are checking in, the baggage is being loaded and the aircraft prepared for departure, the crew arrives for duty at least one hour before takeoff and the captain accepts the aircraft. The flight crew, which may only be a first officer, is briefed by the captain, who will decide who will fly the aircraft on the next leg. It is usually taken in turns, unless one of the crew members is particularly in need of a qualifying leg to fly. The decision as to who is flying the aircraft will also depend on the weather conditions to be met on the route. The route and destination weather report will be studied, as well as any conditions at the departure airport. If the outside conditions are freezing, the decision will need to be made to make sure all ice is removed from the airframe, particularly the aerofoil surfaces such as the wings and tail. Even a thin coating of ice can destroy the vital lift of a wing as well as increasing the weight of the aircraft beyond the takeoff limits. The en-route winds are vital to the flight planning, since a strong headwind will not only delay the flight, but may be beyond the endurance of the planned route, requiring more fuel and less payload. Winds have to be known at all the flight levels to be flown by the aircraft, allowing perhaps the most advantageous altitude to be

Left: *Qantas 737-400 VH-TJW approaches Gate 12 at the Sydney Domestic Terminal.* Philip J. Birtles

217

Above: *The passenger arrival area at Perth International Airport has seats for waiting friends and relatives, and conveniently located rental car desks.* Philip J. Birtles

Left: *The passenger check-in area at Perth International Airport is typical of many international airports, with a row of check-in desks opened for the relevant flights departing within the next three hours. Duty-free shops are located on the floor above.* Philip J. Birtles

selected. The load sheets need to be available to determine not only the overall weight, but also the balance of the aircraft. From this can be derived the takeoff performance, including the speeds related to the decision to abort the takeoff if an engine fails, the rotation speed, and the speed at which the take-off continues even if an engine fails. Whereas this can be critical with a twin-engine airliner, those with three or four engines have a greater margin of safety.

The pilot flying the aircraft will generate the electronic flight plan, and board the aircraft to feed it into the flight data computer. The non-flying pilot will at the same time perform a walk-around while the aircraft is being prepared to ensure that there is no obvious damage. Starting at the nose, he will check the nose wheel tires, brakes, and undercarriage, then inspect the fuselage, making sure that the blanks are removed from the various orifices. The

Above Left: *Malaysia 777-300ER 9M-MRA arrives at Perth International Airport during the early afternoon with the ground handling organization ready to start the turnaround.* Philip J. Birtles

Above: *Malaysia 777-300ER turns toward the airbridge at Perth International Airport, inbound from Kuala Lumpur.* Philip J. Birtles

Left: *Malaysia 777-300ER moves slowly toward the stopping point marked on the ground to match the passenger access door with the airbridge* Philip J. Birtles

inspection will then include the starboard engines, the wing leading edge out to the tip, then the wing trailing edge—including the control surfaces—and finish with the starboard leg of the main undercarriage unit. The walk-around will continue along the starboard side of the fuselage to the tail, where the tailplane and fin, with their respective control surfaces, will be checked for any damage, perhaps caused by a bird strike during the previous flight. Damage can also be inadvertently caused to the fuselage by careless use of the support vehicles, and if the pressure hull is damaged, the aircraft will not be able to maintain pressurization at the cruising altitude. The walk-around continues from the tail back to the front of the aircraft, checking the same areas on the port side. This external walk-around is

not exclusive to commercial airliners, but is a matter of common sense safety for all aircraft operators, from a private pilot to a military jet pilot.

While Captain Bruce Maskeill was performing the walk-around, first officer Paul O'Halloran was entering the flight plan into the flight data computer and running through the checklist to ensure that all the vital systems were functioning. The operation of the aircraft is entirely automatic through the flight data computer, the flight deck crew being computer operators monitoring the functions and feeding in new data when required. A flight can be automatic from takeoff until after landing, but generally the pilots take over control for the final descent, approach, and landing, since greater flexibility is required. Bruce Maskeill is flying the 737 on the flight from Perth to Sydney today, but will let Paul be in command for the next leg.

At 8:45 a.m., the passengers start to board, the cabin being configured for eight business-class passengers and 130 in economy class. The business class is full and there is a total compliment of 144 people on board. In addition to the two members of the flight crew, there are four cabin crew members, with one to look after the refreshments of the business-class passengers and the flight crew, and the other three including the supervisor attending to the economy passengers. If the flight was of a shorter

duration, there would probably be five cabin staff, but the four-hour flight to Sydney allows the full service without rushing, and helps to keep the operation more cost-effective.

At 9:00 a.m., with the loading and refueling completed Flight QF 642 is pushed back from the air bridge by a small tug and positioned on the terminal apron ready to taxi to the runway. The ground crew, who are in radio contact with the flight deck, disconnect and signal to the captain that all the undercarriage locks are removed and the 737 is ready for departure. The flight deck crew runs through the checklist ready for taxiing and the air-

Left: British Airways 747-400 G-CIVR is brought to the departure gate at the Sydney International Terminal ready for preparation for departure. Philip J. Birtles

Below Left: Qantas 747-438 VH-OJF c/n 24483 was delivered in April 1990 and is on the stand ready for preparation for the service to Singapore and Frankfurt. Philip J. Birtles

Below: Qantas 747-438 VH-OJJ is having the containers with baggage and cargo loaded into the forward and rear holds. Philip J. Birtles

craft is directed by ground control to the runway in use, which today is 03, and in the uncongested Perth Airport we are soon cleared onto the runway, ready for departure. The pre-takeoff checklist is run through with the pressure setting for the altimeters (QNH) at 1015, the temperature is a comfortable 23° C (73° F) and there is a 30-knot crosswind. The payload weight is 4,615 lbs., of which about 1,100 lbs. is cargo and mail, bringing the total takeoff weight to 64.3 tons. For departure the decision speed for aborting the takeoff in the event of an engine failure (V1) is 148 knots, the rotate speed (Vr) is 156 knots with takeoff (V2) at 163 knots. Beyond this speed, the aircraft will be capable of a safe climb even if there is an engine failure. There are no clouds, with excellent visibility, and the first officer selects 5 degrees of flap for takeoff with stabilizer trim at 4.7 degrees. Air traffic clears QF 642 for takeoff with an initial clearance up to 6,000 feet, and the 737 begins rolling along the runway, climbing away on track for Sydney.

Once the seat belt signs are switched off, the flight attendants begin the cabin service and

the aircraft climbs to the initial cruising altitude of 29,000 feet. There are no navigation aids along the route, as much of the interior of Australia is arid desert, and some of the route is also over the Great Australian Bight, which is part of the Southern Ocean. Navigation is therefore by inertial reference. Twelve tons of fuel were taken on board at Perth, bringing the total fuel to 14.5 tons, and as it burns off, the aircraft will be cleared to fly at 33,000 feet from about the halfway point in the four-hour journey. Once the cabin service is complete, I am invited up to the flight deck to meet Bruce and Paul and

Left: *Cathay Pacific Airbus A330 is having the catering delivered to the forward and mid galleys using special scissor-jack access vehicles.* Philip J. Birtles

Below Left: *A large pallet is turned through ninety degrees by the special mechanical equipment to present it correctly to the cargo door for loading aboard a Cathay Pacific A330 at Sydney.* Philip J. Birtles

Below: *The large pallet is now on the top platform and ready to be loaded into the hold of a Cathay Pacific A330. Meanwhile, the toilet servicing vehicle is waiting by the nose of the aircraft.* Philip J. Birtles

learn some more about the flight and the crew requirements.

Both Bruce Maskiell and Paul O'Halloran have an ATPL, the promotion to captain being according to seniority and which may take between ten to fifteen years service with the airline. Bruce started work as an engineering apprentice and decided he wanted to fly, so he worked to achieve a CPL. He then spent two years as a charter pilot, gaining experience with bush flying in Queensland. He then flew with a supplemental airline based in Cairns for seventeen years before joining Trans Australian Airlines (TAA) based in Melbourne and flying Boeing 727s. He then converted to Boeing 737s and joined Qantas when it took over TAA, with Melbourne still as his home base. Paul self-financed his own private pilots license (PPL) over a period of four years, eventually gaining an instructor rating. He then joined Qantas International Division as a second officer on Boeing 747-400s, gaining experience over a period of six years. He transferred to domestic flying six years ago, and is also based in Melbourne. Bruce and Paul do not regularly fly

Right: *Pairs of standard containers are next to be loaded into the forward hold of the Cathay Pacific A330 at Sydney.* Philip J. Birtles

Above: *The loading staff maintain a careful check of the loading to ensure that the pallets are boarded in the correct order to ensure a safe balance of the aircraft.* Philip J. Birtles

together and are on average away from base three to four days. Paul made the transfer to domestic flying to avoid longer periods away from home. Both Bruce and Paul are fairly typical pilot entries to Qantas, having invested their own time and money in their future career by starting in general aviation. When necessary, Qantas sponsors flight training by subcontracting to existing flight-training organizations, but do not run its own flight-training school.

The 737-400 is operated by a crew of two, but there is a seat behind the pilots for a check captain or extra crew member. This seat is lowered from a side stowage and has a full five-strap harness. The cockpit has a pair of Attitude Direction Indicators (ADI) on the instrument panel in front of each pilot, with a navigation display below. Both these instruments are digital displays on small flat screen cathode ray tubes (CRT) providing all the necessary information for normal operation of the aircraft. The ADI provides attitude and altitude information, while the navigation display shows the position of the aircraft on the route. The remainder of the instrumentation are the traditional analog dials, the full glass cockpit not being adopted on the 737 until the new generation of aircraft now in production begin worldwide service.

In addition to the normal two wing-mounted engines, there is also an APU mounted in the extreme rear fuselage which normally provides power on the ground for the aircraft systems, air conditioning or warming depending upon the climate, and also power for the engine start. The APU is normally switched on after landing during the taxi to the terminal, and if the aircraft is on a turnaround, it will be kept running until after engine start. In case of an engine failure, normally a twin-jet airliner is only cleared to fly a maximum of sixty minutes flying time on one engine from a suitable diversionary airfield. However, providing the APU is serviceable on departure, supplying a back-up power source for the systems, the Qantas 737-400s are cleared to fly up to 180 minutes from a suitable diversionary airfield. This is known as a 120 minutes Etops, or Extended range Twin-jet OPerationS and is particularly useful across Australia where there are vast areas of featureless desert with no suitable airfields.

The descent for landing at Sydney was commenced twenty minutes before expected touch down with fifty miles to go. The speed was 416 knots and the descent started at between 2,500 and 3,000 feet per minute until 10,000 feet, where the speed was reduced to 250 knots to comply with air traffic requirements. After leveling out at the transition level of 10,000 feet, the descent was continued, and although automatic landing was fitted to the 737, the captain elected to make a manual landing. Still maintaining 250 knots, a turn to starboard was made at 7,000 feet for downwind to runway 34L at Sydney. The descent continues at 1,000 feet per minute, turning to port to acquire the ILS localizer beam lining up with the runway. Flaps are selected at five degrees and the speed brake is deployed to reduce speed to allow the undercarriage to be selected down at 4,500 feet. With three green lights, the undercarriage is locked down and the crew runs through the landing checks with the runway in sight. At 2,000 feet, flaps are selected to ten degrees and there is a Qantas Dash-8 flying to the right on approach to the parallel runway 34R. At 1,000 feet

thirty-degree flaps are selected, and we make a smooth touchdown on the runway, four hours after our departure from Perth. The 737 taxies off the runway at sixty knots and the flaps are retracted, arriving at its assigned stand five minutes after touchdown. The temperature on the ground is a pleasant 91° F (33° C), down from over 108° F (42° C) earlier in the day. During the flight, about eleven tons of fuel have been used, with 7,000 lbs. remaining on board.

While the cabin crew departs for their next assignment, Bruce and Paul complete their shutdown checklist, making sure that everything is switched off and ready for the next crew. They leave this 737 for a 35-minute turnaround on to another 737, which they will fly to Adelaide, and then after another 35-minute turnaround on the same 737, they will fly it to their home base at Melbourne, where their working day will be completed.

The Boeing 737-400 is a second-generation 737 powered by two CFM56-3C-1 turbofan engines developing between 22,000 lbs. (97.9 kN) to 23,500 lbs. (104.5 kN) of thrust each. Qantas has a total of twenty-two in service, together with a further sixteen of the shorter fuselage 737-300s powered by the same engines.

The 737-400 program was launched by Boeing in June 1986 and the first aircraft made the maiden flight from Renton (near Seattle) on February 19, 1988. Certification was achieved for the carriage of up to 188 passengers on September 2 of the same year, with the first delivery on September 15. The 737-400 was developed from the 737-300 by having the fuselage lengthened by 10 feet (3.05 m) with a 6 foot (1.83 m) plug forward of the wing, and another 4 foot (1.22 m) plug behind the wing. The outer wings and undercarriage were also strengthened to cope with the increased gross weight up to 139,000 lbs. (63,050 kg). Although the Qantas 737-400s are normally configured with 139 seats, the 737-400 can carry up to 168 passengers in an all-tourist layout at a maximum takeoff weight of 150,000 lbs. (68,040 kg). The overall length of the fuselage is 119 feet, 7 inches (36.45 m) and the wing span is the same as the 737-300 at 94 feet, 9 inches (28.88 m). Galleys and toilets are located in the forward and aft vestibules.

Cruising speed is at Mach 0.745, with a maximum of Mach 0.82 and the approach speed is 139

229

VH-OGJ

knots. With a full passenger load, the range is 2,090 nautical miles or 2,784 miles/3,870 km.

After a welcome twenty-four hour stopover in Sydney, the time comes for departure on Qantas Boeing 747-400 VH-OJF flight QF 5 from Sydney to Singapore, and then on to Frankfurt. I was fortunate enough to have been able to choose first class for both these long flights, making the journey less of an endurance exercise, and certainly much more restful and enjoyable. Among the advantages are a separate check-in desk, baggage priority on arrival, and a lounge where the passengers can sit quietly and read or work on a computer while taking drinks and light refreshments.

Meanwhile, the 747-400 is being prepared for departure with the catering being loaded, refueling via the under-wing pressure point, and the cargo holds are being carefully loaded with passenger baggage and cargo. The flight crew reports at least one hour before departure to accept the aircraft and undertake the flight briefing. The weather report and satellite charts are supplied, giving the overall pattern over Australia, with further coverage into Asia, including India and the Middle East. Wind speed and direction, as well as air temperature, is charted for flight level 340 over the Asian region from 4:42 p.m. on January 15 until 6:00 a.m. and 12:00 p.m. on January 16. A low-pressure system is expected just after the aircraft passes Brisbane, with another when it approaches Darwin. Although the 747-400 will be cruising at around 35,000 feet, there could be some cumulonimbus clouds with storm centers, which will be desirable to avoid. Local weather reports are supplied for departure from Sydney and arrival at Singapore, together with alternates at Jakarta, Kuala Lumpur, Penang, Den Passar, and Darwin, should the weather at Singapore be unacceptable. The captain briefs for the first officer to fly the Sydney to Singapore leg and also on the flight are two second officers who are traveling to Singapore for other duties, but who

Above Left: One of the pilots performs the preflight walk-around inspection, having just completed the inspection of the starboard turbofan engine on Qantas 767-300ER VH-OGJ at Perth International Terminal. Philip J. Birtles

Left: The pilot's preflight walk-around inspection of Qantas 767-300ER VH-OGJ continues along the starboard wing trailing edge to include the flying controls. Philip J. Birtles

are to be involved in the operation of this flight for additional experience. The electronic flight plan is generated, ready to be loaded into the flight data computer, and the crew is ready to make their way to the Jumbo Jet. As with the 737 flight from Perth, while one pilot does the walk-around to check the external condition of the aircraft, the other is setting up the flight plan and starting to prepare for departure by going through the appropriate checklist. Like the 737-400, the Boeing 747-400 is operated by a crew of two pilots—a captain and a first or second officer. The first officer is fully qualified to fly the aircraft, except to make an automatic landing, which is the responsibility of the captain. As the duration of this flight is about seven hours, there is no requirement to carry a second qualified crew to provide the primary crew with a rest break since the duty time will be well under twelve hours.

With the refueling complete, the catering stowed, and the holds almost loaded, the passengers begin to board, the first-class cabin with fourteen seats being located in the forward section of the aircraft on the main floor, and under the flight deck. Behind the first class section is business class, with a further business-class cabin on the upper deck behind the cockpit totalling sixty-five seats, and the remainder of the main deck is allocated to 315 economy-class passengers. For this flight to Singapore, every seat is full.

As I settle down in my seat, after my jacket is hung in the forward wardrobe, I am offered champagne and water while we wait for the loading to be completed. I have a window seat on the starboard side, although for the latter part of the flight to Singapore, and the twelve-plus hours to Frankfurt, will all be at night, with dawn appearing only when the aircraft is ready for departure from Frankfurt to Heathrow. With the loading complete, the doors are shut and preparations made for the 747 to be pushed back, while the cabin crew demonstrates the emergency procedures, and the empty glasses are collected. The weather at Sydney is cloudy, but dry and pleasantly warm as the Jumbo Jet is taxied alongside the sea wall jutting out into Botany Bay for a takeoff from 34L. Flight QF 5 is cleared for departure from Sydney Airport and climbs away with the famous harbor bridge and opera house on the right, entering clouds over the suburbs of northwest Sydney.

Below: *The four main undercarriage units on the Boeing 747-400 are each fitted with four wheels to spread the load of the aircraft over the concrete. The wheels, tires, brakes, and hydraulic pipes are all checked during the walk-around inspection.* Philip J. Birtles

When the seat belt lights are turned off, a further glass of champagne is offered, and in the interests of research for this book, it is accepted, together with a dish of olives. Because of the continual dehydration, water is also freely available. In due course, canapes are offered and the menu is provided with a selection of three starters and three main courses, plus a selection of excellent Australian wines to complement the food. Each seat is a self-contained unit with individual retractable video screen, folding tables and a fully reclineable seat, which not only has a retractable footrest, but can be made into a bed by linking up with the footrest. The footrest is large enough to be used as an occasional seat for a second person for business discussions or sharing a meal. The catering service for first class comes from the galley in the forward vestibule, where a pair of toilets are also located, one on either side. A toilet bag is issued containing all the items which may be required on the flight, and can be particularly useful at the destination if the passenger's baggage has been lost. When the main meal is ready to be served, a table is pulled up and out of the side wall stowage and laid formally with a cloth, silverware, and appropriate glasses. The food is served on china plates and wine poured from the bottle as in any formal restaurant, unlike the informal economy-class breakfast in a paper bag. Although the flight from Sydney to Singapore was not too late in the day, if a passenger wishes to sleep, the seat is reclined to a bed, with a pillow and blanket available, and pajamas are supplied to allow a change out of the normal daytime travel clothes. It is actually possible to sleep for quite a few hours, making the arrival at the destination less difficult and allowing the possibility of business meetings to be held without any delay.

With the meal service completed, I am invited up to the flight deck where Captain John Dunn is in command with Philip Clode as first officer, the latter flying this sector to Singapore. One of the two first officers, Darryl Sharpe, had made the external

Left: Qantas 747-438 VH-OJJ has completed loading of the cargo and baggage and has a ground power unit plugged into the underside of the nose to provide electrical power in addition to the tail-mounted APU. Philip J. Birtles

walk-around inspection at Sydney, allowing the captain and first officer to make the preparations for the flight in the cockpit. The walk-around inspection is to the same principle as with any other aircraft, but in much greater scale and complexity. Not only are there four engines to inspect, but the main undercarriage consists of four supporting legs each with four wheels, tires, and brakes. The sheer size of the aircraft makes a close inspection of the upper areas more difficult, but this task is nonetheless essential.

When I arrive on the flight deck, the captain is resting with the first officer flying the aircraft from the right-hand seat, assisted by a second officer in the left-hand seat. Although the 747-400 is operated by two pilots, there are two additional seats behind the operating crew for extra crew and check captains, or for passengers like myself with an interest in the operations of the aircraft.

The instrument panel is fitted with a full digital CRT flat screen electronic flight instrument system (EFIS), which consists of a primary flight display (PFD) in front of each pilot. In the case of the left-hand seat, there is a Navigation Display (ND) to the right, which is on the left-hand side of the PFD in the first officer's position. The PFD displays the artificial horizon, which indicates the relative level of the wings in relation to the horizon; the heading, which combines with the wind velocity component to give the actual track; the altitude above mean sea level assuming standard conditions for all aircraft; the indicated airspeed; the Mach number; the vertical speed indicator, which in the cruise should be zero; and the turn and slip indicator which shows the balance of the aircraft, particularly in the turn. An additional piece of information is the target information for the flight director. The ND features a computer-generated moving map showing the aircraft's position in the form of a triangle. The display gives the distance to the next waypoint and a curved

line gives the compass bearing. Ground speed and wind speed and direction are displayed, with an overlay of the signal from the weather radar which can give warning of bad weather ahead. Radio navigation information such as VOR and DME is also available as required.

Between the two pilots in the center of the instrument panel are the two EICAS displays, one above the other, providing essential information of the systems operation during the appropriate phase of flight. The top display is used for the display of engine information, including temperatures and speeds, with any faults being automatically shown. A red alert with an audible warning with the relevant information will signify an important fault which needs immediate attention, while amber is precautionary and green is routine. The central maintenance computer monitors all systems and provides a passive alert if any system malfunctions. In addition, an FDR records all operational parameters to monitor overall performance and assist with the aircraft maintenance. As equipment such as the engines start to show a loss of performance and become less efficient within certain tolerances, maintenance can be scheduled at the next convenient break, to keep the aircraft in the most efficient condition. The screen below has taken over some of the previous systems work of the flight engineer. This display covers all the aircraft systems on eight pages, any of which can be called up to check for any faults. The computer itself is programmed to make any correction or adjustment, recording the problem for repair on the ground. The crew is only kept aware of the information, since there is nothing they can physically do to make any corrections.

The first page on the display covers the full engine parameters, followed by the electric circuits, fuel management, environmental control in the cabin, the hydraulic systems, departure and arrival information, the undercarriage and brakes status and finally, the last page covers general information including the APU functions and control positions.

Captain John Dunn started flying by financing his own PPL, later gaining a CPL, and started work on charter flying. He has now spent thirty years with Qantas, first as a second officer on the Boeing 707s, followed by second officer on the 747-200s, working his way through the first officer duties to qualify as captain of the 747-400. Philip Clode

Above Left: Singapore 777-300ER 9V-SQF is pushed back from the International Terminal at Perth, ready for departure to Singapore. Philip J. Birtles

Left: United 747-400 N191UA is fully loaded and ready to go as it taxies to the runway at Sydney ready for the long oceanic flight across the Pacific to the U.S. Philip J. Birtles

flew about 1,000 hours as a second officer before gaining additional qualifications to be promoted to first officer. Night takeoff and landing criteria are difficult to meet on the long-haul operations and there is a regular cycle on the flight simulator to continue to remain qualified for landings. Philip came from a general aviation background, gaining his PPL, then CPL, followed by a Senior Commercial Pilots License and an Instrument rating, joining Qantas as a second officer; now he has over 8,000 flying hours. One of the second officers, Darryl Sharp, is qualified to fly on 747-400s, 747-200s, and the Boeing 767. New pilots join Qantas from the familiar general aviation route with around 2,000 hours experience, while others may have been to a flying college or come from the Australian Air Force (RAAF). If the ex-RAAF pilots have been jet pilots, the major training task is to help them work as a team rather than try to do it all themselves.

The load on departure was 371 passengers and twenty crew members, with thirty-one tons of cargo, and the passengers and baggage weighing 29.8 tons. Three cabin attendants looked after the first-class cabin, with three more for the upper deck business class, and four in the main deck business cabin. The remainder of the cabin crew served the economy class, with the customer services manager filling in where additional help was needed. The fuel load on the 747-400 at departure was 211,000 lbs., and at the finish of the flight it was expected there would still be 34,000 lbs. of fuel, allowing for a weather diversion to Kuala Lumpur or Jakarta.

Following a standard Sydney departure, the aircraft initially climbed to 28,000 feet, where there was a fair amount of high-altitude cloud and storm activity caused by the low-pressure system. The storm activity showed up on the ND, the red center being the area to avoid, and the course was varied to pass around the thunderstorm activity. As the

Left: *Most of the big airlines run regional jets from their main hubs or have affiliated companies to perform the function. Here a Bombardier Regional Jet of Delta Connection waits with passenger steps lowered at Charleston Airport, South Carolina.* Peter R. March

239

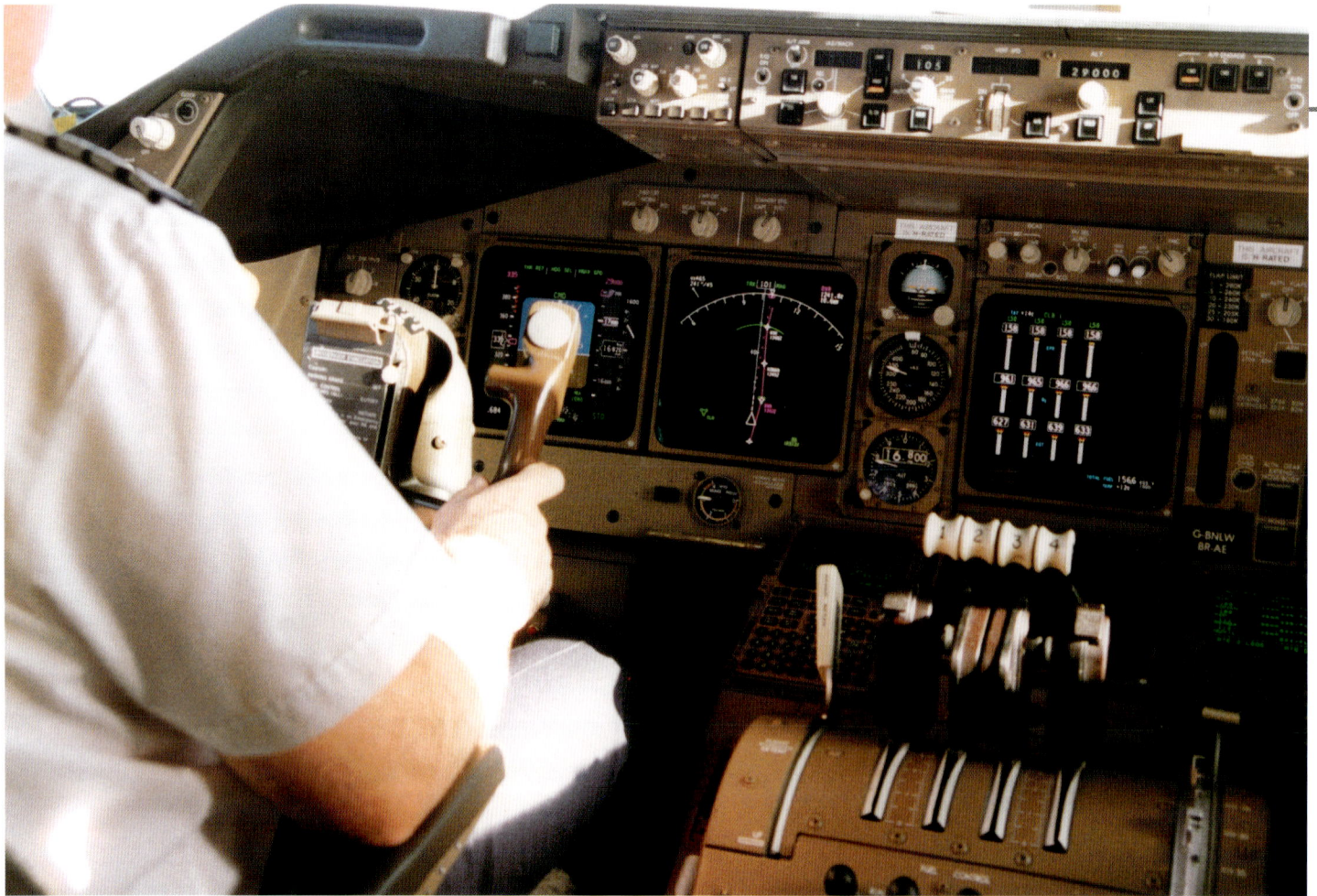

flight progressed, the aircraft would climb to at least 35,000 feet, and maybe even to 39,000 feet. Navigation is by inertial (INS) and electronic GPS which are compared in the navigation computer to maintain the desired course. Communication is done by HF radio to Perth and Bali flight information services (FIS), in addition to satellite communications and a data link with the base in Sydney. As it is still line-of-sight, there were also VHF communications with Brisbane as well as a data link. Although the 747-400 is flying automatically throughout the journey, the crew is constantly inputting new data to ensure that there is no conflict with other aircraft on the airway, particularly if there are aircraft at a similar level which could be overtaken, or could catch up with the flight.

Ann Maree Morrison applied for the position of customer services manager (CSM) three years ago after working with Qantas for seventeen years, and is assisted by a supervisor. Cabin staff can apply for the position after seven years of service, but they are not promoted automatically. The final appointment depends on seniority and years of service with Qantas, as well as their suitability for the job. All the cabin crew have an annual medical and license which is validated annually by an emergency procedures check. To maintain the quality of service, there may be an oral exam for any member of the crew before each flight, with at least one due to every cabin crew member every two to four weeks to check their safety awareness. An assessment form is also completed after every trip for all the cabin crew to provide immediate feedback on their performance in the safety aspects, as well as on their customer-service skills.

The cabin crew can work up to fourteen hours, and even that can be extended, but usually with the possibility of some rest during a quiet period of the flight. After every flight, there is at least twelve

Above Left: On the 747-400 flight deck, in front of the captain is the PFD with the ND to the right. In the center of the panel is the top screen of two of the EICAS displays. The four engine thrust levers obscure the lower EICAS. Philip J. Birtles

Left: Typical of the Boeing 777-200 economy-class cabin are nine abreast seats with individual seat-back video screens for the passenger entertainment system. Philip J. Birtles

hours of rest, but this depends upon the next assignment. The cabin crews are assigned independently of the flight crews, and do not operate as a single crew, but vary as the need arises. The Qantas cabin crews are qualified to operate on the airline's Boeing 747SP, -200s, -300s, and −400s, as well as on the Boeing 767-200/300s. Because of the close working relationship with British Airways, they are also qualified to work on the BA 747-400s and 767-300s, some of the latter also being on lease to Qantas.

Like most of the other long-haul crews, Ann Maree is based in Sydney, but because she has a three hour drive from home, she prefers the longer periods away. On this particular duty, she expects to be away for around ten days, but it could vary from eight to fifteen days. She would then have between three and five nights at home depending upon the intensity of the assignments. While away, to try to maintain some level of rest, the crews will often stay on their original local time. The crew members will retire to their hotel and sleep, whatever the local time, ready to start afresh with a new crew on the next flight to which they are assigned.

As already mentioned, the prime duty of the cabin crew is to maintain the safety of the passengers, and they have to be constantly alert with continual monitoring of the cabins. In the early days of airline travel, the cabin crew would also be responsible for serving some light refreshments, but with the increased competitive environment, attempts are constantly being made to improve the product to attract new customers and also retain the loyalty of the current passengers. One of the major promotional items is the logging of air miles, which can be used at a later date for a leisure journey, an example being this writer's trip to Australia. Other options are companion vouchers earned by regular travelers, which can allow a partner to travel with the regular customer to whatever destination they are booked. For example, this can be used for anything from a business-class trip to Hong Kong to an economy-class flight to Paris.

On board the aircraft itself, changes to the product are made which can take up to two years to implement, and where appropriate the cabin crew is trained to operate the new features. Seats and meals are probably of the greatest concern to passengers, particularly on long flights. The airlines earn the

10

most return from the premium-class passengers in first-class and business-class cabins. With the gradual introduction of first-class seats which convert into beds, a similar type of seat is now being introduced into the business-class cabins, but with less surrounding space and a less exotic, but adequate, menu. With the lower cost of traveling economy, to maintain an effective overall yield, the seating has to be more dense. Most airlines are aware that sometimes an executive will travel business class for work to maintain effectiveness after arriving at the destination, but when flying for leisure, may downgrade to economy class. Airlines also realize that today's economy-class passenger could be tomorrow's premium-class passenger.

For short flights, meals are not often required, but usually light refreshments and beverages are usually offered. Great care is taken with the menus for the premium-class passengers, and the meals served in economy class are usually adequate, with alcohol included on international flights. After a long journey, it is an enjoyment to be able to eat anything but airline food, since in most cases airline food is used as a way to keep the passengers occupied.

Another innovation in recent years has been the development of passenger entertainment systems, changing from the original communal screens in the cabin to individual seat-back or armrest-mounted screens. For premium passengers, there can be a choice of videos to watch, and the rest of the passengers have a choice of movies, as well as music and other entertainment. Safety and operational announcements by the crew can also be made through the system. These passenger entertainment systems have taken many years to perfect, as the data is fed to the seat via contacts in the standard seat rails on the cabin floor. As already mentioned,

apart from the first-class cabin, the seating, galleys and toilet layout can be rearranged overnight, as all units are mounted on seat rails, making correct connection essential for trouble-free service. With the continual advances in electronics, it is essential that the passenger entertainment system is compatible with the many other electronics and avionics installed in the aircraft. With sophisticated fly-by-wire piloting, flight computers, and other advanced systems, everything needs to be working in harmony. If the passenger entertainment system has not been installed and tested by the manufacturer of the aircraft, there could be significant difficulties with the installation. In some cases this has resulted in a total abandonment of a particular system, to be replaced by a new one, at enormous cost across the airline fleet.

Left: *To cope with the average carry-on bags, the overhead luggage bins on the Boeing 777 have been made larger, a feature which can be achieved easier in the more spacious wide-body jet airliner cabins.* Philip J. Birtles

Right: *With ACARS now being downloaded by satellite, in addition to the engineering and operational data being sent to the airline operations department, passengers can make use of sky-phones for communications with the ground.* Philip J. Birtles

Most passengers are not overly concerned about the general trim and décor, but with the need to bring into the cabin large carry-on bags— including documents and possibly a laptop computer— stowage can be a challenge. The newer cabin interiors are now being configured with large overhead bins to take even the most stubborn carry-on bag. To ensure that there is no overload, some airlines insist that a carry-on bag fits into a size gauge, and if it is too large, it is consigned to the baggage hold. The writer always plans to carry at least a toilet kit on board to ensure that in the event of the luggage being lost, at least it will be possible to freshen up.

The majority of passengers are those who fly on holiday with an inclusive tour, with the major criteria being the lowest possible cost. As a result, there is little choice of products aboard the aircraft, although journeys are becoming longer and passengers may be prepared to pay a premium to arrive at the destination without being exhausted.

Qantas has a fleet of thirty-six Boeing 747s, of which twenty-four are 747-400s. While the earlier versions can be operated by common crews, including a flight engineer to look after the systems, the two-crew 747-400 requires special training. Pilots from the Efis-equipped two-crew 767 fleet may find it easier to adapt to the techniques of operating the newer aircraft. Although the 747-300 is visually similar to the 747-400, it does not have the main recognition feature of drag-reducing winglets at the wingtips. The Qantas 747-400s typically carry up to 396 passengers with 31,500 lbs. of cargo, or 373 passengers with 32,200 lbs. Up to 524 passengers can be carried by a 747-400 in a mixed business-class and economy configuration.

The Boeing 747 Jumbo Jet was launched into production after an order for twenty-five aircraft

Right: *On the completion of the flight, the Qantas 747-400 approaches to land. In this case it is 747-438 VH-OJH which was delivered to Qantas in August 1990 and is approaching to land at London Heathrow in June 2000. The undercarriage is down, the flaps are at twenty degrees, and the 747-400 recognition feature is the upturned winglets, which Qantas paints red.* Philip J. Birtles

The Journey

from Pan American Airlines on April 13, 1966. The first flight was on February 9, 1969, and following certification on December 30 of the same year, it entered service on the New York to London route on January 22, 1970. The first of the large wide-body long-range jet airliners, the 747 brought new levels of productivity and economics, allowing more competitive fare structures and making air travel affordable for more people. The 747-400 development was announced in October 1985 with extended range and capacity, with the first production example making the maiden flight on April 29, 1988. The aircraft was certified with three different types of turbofan engines and Qantas adopted the Rolls-Royce RB211 as originally developed for the Lockheed TriStar. The first delivery was to Northwest Airlines on January 26, 1989. Qantas ordered their first four 747-438s in 1987 with options on a further fifteen aircraft, and the first was delivered on August 17, 1989, having flown nonstop from London Heathrow to Sydney. The aircraft flew the 9,720 nautical miles in just over twenty hours, using 179.5 tons of fuel, with four tons remaining on arrival. The aircraft carried eighteen people, including a crew of four Qantas pilots and one from Boeing, and had a fully furnished interior, but with reduced galley equipment.

The four Rolls-Royce RB211 turbofan engines develop 58,000 lbs. of thrust each and are mounted in pods under pylons located on the wing leading edge. The overall length of the aircraft is 231 feet, 10 inches (70.66 m) and the wing span is 211 feet, 5 inches (64.44 m). The maximum takeoff weight is 875,000 lbs. A typical design range is 7,135 nautical miles (13,214 km or 8,211 miles). The maximum cruise speed is 611 mph, which is equivalent to Mach 0.85; the approach speed is 176 mph and the maximum cruise altitude is 45,000 feet.

Above Left: *Aer Lingus Premier class on an A330.* Peter R. March

Left: *The 2 x 3 cabin of a Boeing 717—Boeing's name for what had been developed as the McDonnell Douglas MD-95. The 717 is a short to medium-range airliner that can carry around 100 passengers some 1,500 miles at a service ceiling of 36,000 feet.* Peter R. March

On a typical flight from Sydney to Singapore, the aircraft will fly across New South Wales, then between Queensland and South Australia, across the vast red arid deserts of Northern Territories and leave the coast of Western Australia close to Derby in the northwest. The route then passes Indonesia past Borneo, Java, and Sumatra to arrive at Singapore.

The captain runs through his briefing on the flight deck to ensure that there is a complete understanding in the event of any emergency on departure and all preparations and checks are completed for departure. The local airfield information has been received and the passenger-access air bridge is moved clear of the aircraft. A call is made to Sydney ground control, giving the call sign and position on stand, requesting permission for engine start and push-back and taxi to runway 34L, where we had landed the previous day in the 737-400. With the clearance for push-back received, the brakes are released and autostart is selected for engine numbers 4 and 3, followed by 2 and 1. The aircraft beacons are switched on and all the main deck access doors, which are also emergency exits, are switched to automatic. In the event of an emergency, when the doors are opened the safety slides will automatically deploy for passenger escape.

With a clearance to taxi, the aircraft begins to move and the pre-takeoff checks are completed, confirming that the controls are full and free, flaps set at twenty degrees, trim set and the transponder checked. The cockpit is a considerable height above the ground, with the nose wheel immediately below the crew, and it is important to have adequate clearance all around, assisted by the yellow center lines along the taxiway. Not only is it essential to give clearance for the wing tips, but when turning, the massive tail swings around and the turbofan engines generate a high volume of jet blast. As the aircraft approaches the holding point at the end of the runway, the captain calls that they are ready for departure. Air traffic gives the clearance for departure after the arrival of a Qantas 767, which can be seen approaching over Botany Bay. Once the 767 has landed, we are cleared on to the runway and told to wait while the 767 clears. We are then cleared for takeoff to an initial altitude of 5,000 feet and the power is increased as we start rolling along the runway with V1 at 151 knots, Vr at 155 knots, and

V2 at 162 knots. The aircraft climbs away over Sydney with the undercarriage retracting, and the communications are made with Sydney radar control. As the aircraft passes through 1,000 feet, the retraction of the flaps commences, first to ten degrees, then five degrees, and finally fully up. As the aircraft climbs, a speed check is called to ensure that we are well clear of the stalling speed. Once clear of Sydney and established in a climb, a call is made to Sydney radar for the departure procedure and joining of the airway.

A modern airliner is a very expensive capital asset to buy and operate. However, when it is flying it has the potential of making a profit, whereas on the ground it does not generate revenue for the airline. Airliners are usually in the control of a number of crews over the period of time it is away from its base. In the past the only communications were with the local station managers through VHF radio, which can only be used for the briefest messages to avoid clogging valuable airwave time. With the development of more sophisticated avionics, there are more efficient methods of downloading important data in real time.

The main task of an airline operations department is to maximize the cost-effectiveness of the fleet, ideally by tracking each individual aircraft, and meeting repair needs if a problem arises. As in most industries, aviation has its fair share of jargon, and one of these is "oooitimes," used by the operations department to identify one of their prime needs—out, off, on, in time. This identifies the times for chocks away, takeoff, landing, and on chocks. Piedmont Airlines in the U.S. was the first airline in the world to use real-time "oooitimes" at their operations center in 1977 through the use of ACARS, which is an Arinc aeronautical digital communications system. By installing switches on various operational parts of the aircraft, such as the main entry door, parking brakes, and main undercarriage, messages can be sent by datalink to the home base, keeping track of the aircraft movements. ACARS is established world wide on all the major trunk routes covering North America, Europe, the Middle East, central and southeast Asia, and Australasia. It is managed in the U.S. by Arinc, Canada by Air Canada and by the Sita network in the rest of the world. These management systems are fully compatible and are linked to each other to maintain the most comprehensive coverage.

The two major reasons for choosing an ACARS system is for operations-driven and engineering-driven information, the combined information being desirable for the overall efficient management of the fleet. The initial use of ACARS in the U.S. was largely operations-driven, but Europe and Australia have been able to take advantage of the system by introducing it later when it was more mature, allowing a wider information service with no boundary limits. It was the introduction of digital aircraft, such as the Boeing 747-400, Boeing 777, and the Airbus family from the A320 onward which made the aircraft more compatible with the new communications system. These aircraft are already equipped with aircraft conditioning/monitoring systems (ACMS), digital airworthiness recorders (DAR), and built-in test equipment (BITE), giving a capacity for continually monitoring the health of the aircraft systems in real time. Any pilot-reported information may only be transmitted briefly during the flight, or after arrival at the destination, with the detailed technical data downloaded when convenient. However, the computers on modern airliners can analyze far more information than the operating crew, and transmit it in a fraction of the time. The aircrew can only report a problem after it occurs, rather than prevent it from happening—which diagnostic computers can help to achieve. Although the normal air-traffic VHF frequencies are used for ACARS data flow, the messages are sent and received in digital format, cutting transmission time to a fraction of a second, greatly increasing the amount of information which can be exchanged. Voice communications on a long-haul operation using the company frequency tend to be one or two per flight, while ACARS generates over twenty messages per flight with the data being of much higher quality. When received, the information can either be displayed on a VDU or in printed form while the

Above Left: *Loading luggage onto a Qantas Boeing 767 at Sydney Airport.* Peter R. March

Left: *Passenger gangway connected to a Boeing 737 of Thai Airlines at Bangkok.* Peter R. March

Right: *Manchester Visual Control Room*. NATS

Below: *Aberdeen Approach Controllers*. NATS

ground and aircraft computers are communicating directly.

When using ACARS for engineering data, there is enough computing power on board the aircraft to carry out performance monitoring, which could previously only be done on the ground. The results can be downloaded in real time, whereas previously the could take up to five days to analyze, possibly too late for any remedial action to be taken to fix a fault before permanent damage was done. Using engine health monitors (EHM), trouble can be anticipated, and a solution devised by computer. This not only improves safety, but gives cost savings in terms of mechanical damage and aircraft downtime. Preventive maintenance, the insurance against breakdowns, can be planned and targeted with greater precision, reducing costs while maintaining safety levels. Any defective parts can be detected in flight and a replacement can be available for the arrival of the aircraft at the next destination.

Although ACARS is ideal to incorporate in the new digital airliners, modification of earlier aircraft is not difficult in hardware terms. The major challenge is to develop the software to program the older, more engineering-intensive aircraft into the overall fleet maintenance schedule. The system can lead to faster turnarounds, more efficient maintenance and better aircraft utilization, as well as bringing further passenger service improvements.

To meet busy departure slots for the congested airways, the aircraft needs to depart on schedule, or face delays of up to two hours. One of the most common reasons for missing slots is the late arrival of the load sheet due to the arrival of last-minute passengers or cargo. Until the captain sees and approves the load sheet, the doors cannot be closed for departure. Often the taxi time to the departure runway can be quite lengthy, and if the aircraft is equipped with an on-board Aircom printer, the captain can receive the load sheet while in the takeoff line, and certainly before takeoff clearance is given. The oooitimes can also include a "nearly there" signal from landing lights, radio altimeter and flaps, which allows the most efficient deployment of ramp personnel and equipment for the arrival.

Air traffic control clearances, which are often long and complex, can be passed by ACARS to a flight deck printer, reducing the chances of error and avoiding VHF clutter caused by transmitting the clearance and the read-back. Routine information such as aerodrome terminal information service (ATIS) can be received by the crew and read at the appropriate time, together with a last-minute update of the weather at the destination and alternates. To overcome the limitations of the VHF line-of-sight transmissions, ACARS is now satellite-linked to cover remote areas of the world or oceanic routes not covered by ground stations. The satcom system involves a tenfold increase in installation costs but provides global coverage and allows passengers to make use of sky phones. Digital downlinks via satellite give access to computer reservation systems, providing rapid confirmation for passenger travel, hotel reservations, and rental car bookings. Longer-term developments are expanding flight operations and adding cabin management, the latter including catering needs, transfer assistance, local information, and passenger messages. This has been developed as an evolutionary process, but brings a revolution in the efficient operation of an air transport system.

The 747-400 has now reached the point where the descent into Singapore has started its pass over Indonesia. The crew begins their descent briefing and we will be under radar control for landing on runway 02L. The descent briefing covers our safety altitude and the transition level. A check is made for any problems, of which there are none, and the weather conditions at the destination will not cause any problems with the approach, although we will be landing in the dark. The runway state is dry and we will use reverse thrust and autobraking as standard. The safety altitude is between 1,700 and 2,000 feet and the final approach will be made down the ILS glide slope and localizer manually by the first officer. In the event of a need to abandon the landing and go around, the decision height is 220 feet with the flaps set at twenty degrees with a positive climb on the flight director to 1,100 feet. The undercarriage will then be raised and the climb continued to 3,000 feet with the flaps raised to five degrees and the climb speed to be ten knots above the minimum. With the briefing completed, the descent/approach checks are made, covering: Recall —checked, briefing—complete, VREF—set, minima—set, and the altimeters QNH cross-checked after the transition level. A call is made to Singapore approach, who transfer the flight to Singapore

Radar and at the top of the descent the air speed is Mach 0.77 with a ground speed of 448 knots. A descent is given to 10,000 feet, followed by a further descent to 6,000 feet on a heading for 02L. Fifteen minutes from touchdown, the seat belt lights are turned on and the cabin crew is asked to take their seats after preparing for landing. The leading edge slats are lowered to provide extra lift and at 4,000 feet, about seventeen miles from touchdown, the autopilot is disconnected, the aircraft now being flown by hand for the first time since the start of the takeoff run.

With the aircraft established on the approach, a change of frequency is made to Singapore Tower, with the flaps set at twenty degrees and the undercarriage lowered. The approach lights are in sight and the landing checklist is followed: speedbrake—armed, autobrakes—set, landing gear—down, flaps—twenty degrees, cabin crew—report received. The landing checks are complete.

We are given clearance to land by the ATC and the speed brake is selected and the main flaps are lowered to twenty-five degrees as we come in over the airport boundary, with the heights being called above the runway. We touch down at 00.40 hrs Sydney time, which is 9:40 p.m. locally, the flight time being seven hours and ten minutes. After touchdown, the reverse thrust is selected, slowing the aircraft to taxiing speed, and the radio is changed to Singapore Ground, who directs us to the assigned airbridge in Terminal 1. The weather radar is turned off and the APU is started in preparation for providing ground power. While the first officer continues to taxi to the terminal, the captain is running through the after-landing checks: strobes—off, stabilizer—six units, speed-brake—down, flaps—up, APU electrics—available. As the arrival is made to the airbridge, the call is made to the cabin crew to switch the doors to manual to avoid the activation of the emergency chutes. As the airbridge moves out to connect with the passenger exit, the brakes are on, switches are off and the chocks are located under the nose wheels. The shut-down checklist covers: hydraulic demand pumps—off, fuel pump switches—off, weather radar—off, park brake—as required, fuel control switches—cut off.

This flight, which could have been two years in preparation, is now complete, but it does not stop there. Having arrived at Singapore, the aircraft is prepared for the next leg to Frankfurt, keeping pace with the continual darkness until some three hours after arrival. Captain John Dunn said that a flight is like a bridge. Few people are interested how it is designed, built, and maintained—they just want to use it.

Left: *KLM 747-300 Combi at on a wet and foggy day at Schipol.*
Brian S. Strickland

Glossary

ACARS	Aircraft communication addressing and reporting system
ACMS	Aircraft conditioning monitoring systems
ADF	Automatic direction finder
ADI	Attitude direction indicators
AMSL	Above mean sea level
APU	Auxiliary power unit
ATC	Air traffic control(ler)
ATIS	Aerodrome terminal information service
ATR	Avion de Transport Régional
ATP (L)	Air transport pilot's license
BA	British Airways
BAC	British Aircraft Corporation
BAe	British Aerospace
CAA	Civil Aviation Authority (U.K.)
CNS/ATM	Communication, navigation, surveillance and air traffic management
CPT (L)	Commercial transport pilot's license
CRT	Cathode ray tube
CSM	Customer services manager
CSWAFC	China Southern West Australia Flying College
CTPL	Commercial transport pilot's license
CVR	Cockpit voice recorder
DDRMI	Digital distance and radio magnetic indicator
DVT	Deep vein thrombosis
ECS	Environmental control system
EFIS	Electronic flight instrument system
EHM	Engine health monitor
EICAS	Engine indicating and crew alerting system
EPR	Engine pressure ratio
ER	Extended range
F	Freighter
FAA	Federal Aviation Authority (U.S.)
FCU	Flight control unit
FDR	Flight data recorder
FIGI	Flight/ground instructor test
FIS	Flight information services
FL	Flight level
FMC	Flight management computer
FOI	Fundamentals of instructing

GE	General Electric
GNSS	Global navigation satellite system
GPS	Global positioning system
GPWS	Ground proximity warning system
IATA	International Air Transport Association
ICAO	International Civil Aviation Organization
IFR	Instrument flight rating
ILS	instrument landing system
INMARSAT	International Maritime Satellite
INS	Inertial navigation system
IR	Instrument rating
JAA	Japanese Aviation Authority
LCD	Liquid crystal display
LR	Long-range
MFDU	Multi-function display units
NATS	National Air Traffic Services Limited (Britain)
Navaid	navigation aid
ND	Navigation display
NJS	National Jet Systems
nm	Nautical mile
P&W	Pratt & Whitney
PFD	Primary flight display
PPL	Private pilot's license
QFE	Local air pressure
QNH	Air pressure
RJ	Regional jet
SATCOM	Satellite communication
SATNAV	Satellite navigation
SELCAL	Selective calling
SID	Standard instrument departure
STARS	Standard arrival routes
STOL	Short take-off and landing
TAA	Trans Australian Airlines
TCAS	Traffic collision avoidance system
V1	Decision speed for aborting the takeoff in the event of an engine failure
V2	Takeoff
VFR	Visual Flight Rating
VOR	Very high frequency omnirange
Vr	The speed at which an aircraft's nose wheel lifts off the runway

Right: *Busy day at Delta's home base, Atlanta International Airport.* Peter R. March

Index